BISON
BOOKS

LETTERS HOME

Henry Matrau

OF THE

IRON BRIGADE

EDITED

By Marcia Reid-Green

FOREWORD

By Reid Mitchell

University of Nebraska Press

Lincoln & London

⊗ The paper in this book meets the minimum require-
ments of American National Standard for Information
Sciences – Permanence of Paper for Printed Library
Materials, ANSI z39.48-1984.

First Bison Books printing: 1998
Most recent printing indicated by
the last digit below:
10 9 8 7 6 5 4 3 2 1

Library of Congress Cataloging-in-Publication Data
Matrau, Henry, 1845-1917.
Letters home: Henry Matrau of the Iron Brigade /
edited by Marcia Reid-Green; foreword by Reid Mitchell.
p.   cm.   Includes bibliographical references and index.
ISBN 0-8032-3151-2 (cl.: alkaline paper)
ISBN 0-8032-8242-7 (pbk.: alkaline paper)
1. Matrau, Henry, 1845-1917 – Correspondence.
2. United States. Army. Iron Brigade (1861-1865) –
Biography.   3. United States – Civil
War, 1861-1865 – Personal narratives.
4. Soldiers – United States – Correspondence.
1. Reid-Green, Marcia, 1936-   II. Title.
E492.4.176M38   1993   973.7′8-dc20
92-26862   CIP

Contents

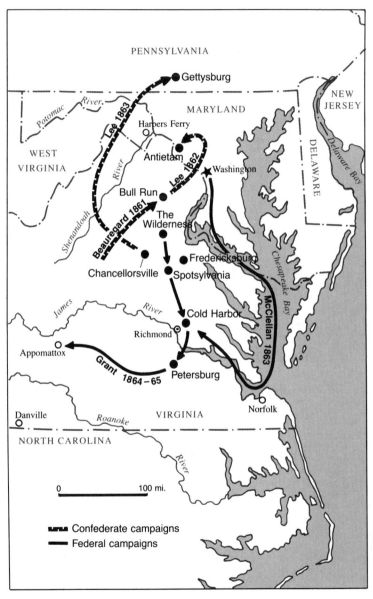

Major Campaigns in the Eastern Theater of the Civil War, 1861–1865

Foreword

HE CAME from a small town in Michigan. He was born in 1845, so he was only sixteen years old when he snuck and lied his way into the Union Army. Like many of his fellow soldiers, he was the son of a farmer. The rhetoric of an industrial North and an agrarian South shouldn't mislead us: the Union Army depended largely on small-towners and country boys like Henry Matrau. In his hometown, the recruiting agents of the newly forming volunteer Union Army knew perfectly well that Henry was too young to enlist; Henry had to go where he was not known to join the army. Even after he finally succeeded, in Beloit, Wisconsin, his age, or at least his appearance, was commented on; he became known as "the Baby of Company G." He left the army, in his own words, a "young, weather beaten, tanned, old veteran." He rose from private to captain in four years. He also wrote the letters home that compose this book. They were not written incidentally or casually. They were the means by which he shared his feelings and thoughts with the ones he loved best. Henry Matrau did not write them for you or for me to read. Yet by reading them, and the letters of other men and women of the Civil War era, we obtain the most personal and most heartfelt picture of those times.

Historians have not exactly neglected soldiers' letters and

diaries. In the 1930s, Lloyd Lewis began to see how regimental histories, many of which incorporated soldiers' letters, could be used to paint a fuller picture of the Civil War experience. He was followed in this by the better-known Bruce Catton, whose Army of the Potomac trilogy provided a model of how to combine the experience of the rank-and-file soldier with traditional military history told from the general's point of view. But not every historian was interested in using letters and diaries to address the questions of battles and campaigns, tactics and strategy. Bell I. Wiley, with his pioneering *Life of Johnny Reb* and its successor, *The Life of Billy Yank*, focused almost exclusively on the concerns of the common soldier — what he ate and wore, how he marched and lived and fought, what he fought for. If there can be any complaint about Bell Wiley's treatment of the Union and the Confederate soldier, it would have to be about his originality, thoroughness, and reputation. What he wrote was so good that it took a generation before historians permitted themselves to reexamine the soldier experience in detail.

When they did — I should say, when we did — they did so for many reasons. The ongoing fascination and relevance of the Civil War, its capacity to serve as a representation of the best and worst of the United States and its past, its simultaneity of comedy, epic, and tragedy — all of these drew in professional historians because we are humans even before we are historians. But there were two additional reasons for the renewed interest in Civil War soldiers. First, many of us were influenced by trends in the study of American history at large, the "new social history." During the 1960s and 1970s, historians felt increasingly compelled to find out about the lives of American men and women who had not dominated the politics and institutions of their times: in short, the average man and the average woman.

Investigating the lives of these men and women — unfortunately and inaccurately labeled the "inarticulate" — became not only a research project but a matter of more than academic dedication on the part of many historians. In their search for the inarticulate, the new social historians invented and employed many innovative methods. But the letters and diaries of Civil War soldiers offered an opportunity to hear the inarticulate, so-called, in all their many voices: plain or fancy; romantic, cynical, or disillusioned; and frequently powerful and moving.

Second, the 1970s saw a shift in the field of military history itself toward what some have dubbed "the New Military History" but what I prefer to call the study of war as it relates to society. Two very different books helped create this new approach to military history. The first, Paul Fussell's *The Great War and Modern Memory*, discussed, among a great many other things, the impact of the war in the trenches on the psyche of soldiers and junior officers. The second, John Keegan's *Face of Battle*, tried to recreate what the experience of battle was like for the individual soldier. Keegan in particular led military historians back to the experience of the soldier as part of the fundamentals of their craft.

What were we looking for? We were looking for answers to questions that Bell Wiley had not asked or had not asked in ways that sounded urgent enough to us. Is it sufficient to simply point to the troubling willingness of the Civil War generation to accept that war's death toll as a sign of patriotism, when we suspect that would demoralize us to the point we could not make war? Gerald Lindermann in *Embattled Courage* decided no. He investigated what Civil War soldiers meant by courage, why they were so devoted to it, and how their definition changed during the war years. Could we continue to celebrate the patriotism, bravery, and endurance of Civil War soldiers and avoid hard questions about what they were fighting for? Earl Hess wrote *Liberty, Virtue, and Progress* to analyze the ideology behind the Northern war effort. Could we write about Civil War soldiers and ignore the fact that there was a sizable component of the Union Army that was black? Joseph Glathaar's most recent book, *Forged in Battle*, addressed the relationship between the Union soldier's black soldiers and their white officers. Could we accept the similarities between Johnny Reb and Billy Yank and not question how and why people who shared a common identity as Americans chose to organize mass armies and slaughter one another? Randall Jimerson's *A People Divided* and my own *Civil War Soldiers* returned to the theme of "a brother's war." All of us looked to soldiers' letters, diaries, and memoirs to understand why individuals north and south made the decisions they did and how they endured the consequences of those decisions.

The documents that historians of the soldiers' experience use are the ones that make up this book. Nobody is really *an average man*. Henry Matrau, the author of the letters you are about to read, certainly wasn't. But in many ways, his experience of the war, its hardships, and its meaning are comparable to the experiences of a lot of other Union soldiers and not a few Confederate ones. We can see in his life many of the patterns elucidated by recent historians while also acknowledging his own irreducible, human uniqueness. We can take Henry Matrau as a representative of all Union soldiers but only if we recognize that first and foremost he was Henry Matrau.

What impelled this very young man to serve four hard and dangerous years in the Union Army? Nowhere in his letters does he speak directly to what caused him to serve and fight and risk his life. Perhaps he had already discussed his reasons with his parents. I wonder. Nothing indicates Henry was vocal and many of us make our most important choices reluctant or unable to give explanations. The one thing that becomes clear when you read his letters is that he went because he thought it his duty.

The young Henry Matrau either was not a reflective man or was unwilling to share his reflections with others. His letters home rarely discuss the ideological or political issues of the day. The fact that his letters devote little space to the Union, Emancipation, or Reconstruction should not mislead us into thinking Matrau lacked convictions. From the way he backed his convictions, they seem to have been deeply felt if rarely expressed. He once explained to his parents, "Politics dont trouble us here in the Army much[.] the most we think about is whether the rebellion can be put down or not[.]"

Presumably Matrau grew up in a Whig family; his parents named him after Henry Clay. It seems likely that once that party declined and the Republicans were organized, the Matraus supported the new party. In any case, their eldest son, Henry, joined the Union Army before he was old enough to vote and voted — like the majority of soldiers — for Lincoln when he had the chance in 1864. "I put in a straight Republican ticket myself," he said. "I thought I had served my Uncle Samuel long enough to entitle me to have a word to say about who is to run the machine."

Notions of manhood and duty also determined Henry's conduct. Writing from the army, he commented on the young men back home who might want to avoid the draft. "Any young man who is drafted now and forgets his manhood so far as to hire a substitute is'nt worthy the name of man and ought to be put in petticoats immediately." When his brother Frank enlisted, he was philosophical. "Soldiering teaches one hard lessons," he advised his parents, "but they will last a man his life time."

On slavery, emancipation, and race, Matrau was oddly silent. Many Northern soldiers took great interest in the South's peculiar institution, sending home reports and judgments. Matrau mentioned blacks only once: "We were on picket the other side of Fall's Church last week but didn't meet with any remarkable adventures other than the capture of 4 Contrabands who we delivered up to Uncle Sam their rightful owner." The promulgation of the Emancipation Proclamation — a matter of considerable discussion among Union and Confederate soldiers alike — passed by without a comment or even a mention from Matrau. Even though he described the Battle of the Crater in some detail, he never once mentioned that one of the divisions in the Union assault was black. In fact, he never mentioned seeing a black man in uniform.

Matrau exhibited the enthusiasm for battle, as well as the considerable naiveté, associated with volunteer soldiers at the start of the war. Before McClellan's Peninsula campaign in spring, 1862, Matrau wrote home, "When we start it is'nt likely that we'll stop far this side of Bull's Run and McLellan will do his best to smoke out that nest of hornets. He will storm Manassas at the point of the bayonet. and to make us proficient in the art of punching our fellow man we have been for the last month drilling in the bayonet exercise." Not only did Matrau guess wrong about the object of McClellan's innovative campaign, but he overestimated, even romanticized, the bayonet, a tool that soldiers soon dismissed as practically useless. Matrau admitted that perhaps he and his fellow soldiers should have some moral qualms about battle — "It is strange what a predeliction we have for injuring our brother man but we learn the art of killing far easier than we do a hard problem in arithmetic" — but he anticipated battle with eagerness. "All are anxious to move and the boy's look smiling enough when there is any chance for a scrummage."

That was the voice of the volunteer soldier who had not yet been in battle. We hear the voice of the veteran after Matrau has watched the slaughter-pen that was the battle of Fredericksburg. "The paper's all say that the soldiers are aching to fight but the papers are notorious liars." Later on, discouraging his brother Morgan from enlisting, he writes, "Take my word for it though I'll own it aint romantic[:] a good soldier cares more for a good meal than he does for all the glory he can put in a bushel basket." Morgan, by the way, was not discouraged, at least not permanently; he enlisted less than a year later.

Matrau's battles were far from over; the Iron Brigade suffered heavier casualties than any other brigade in the Union Army. At Gettysburg Matrau reports, "The best hearted fellow in our company was killed right close to me so near that he nearly fell on to me." At the Battle of the Wilderness, his brigade "fought all the forenoon[,] gained nothing & lost nothing but men." Indeed, young Matrau's attitude toward the army is one thing that sets him apart from most of his fellow soldiers. Having made officer, he wanted to persist in the military life whereas most Yankees wanted to go home. Nevertheless, he viewed his war-weary fellow veterans — "the men who perilled fortune, life, and limb to sustain the republic — as their nation's proven support. Even though they were eager now for their discharges and resentful that they were long in coming, "in six months after they are discharged these same men they are using so badly now will forget all this & enlist to help their country as willingly as they did in 1861[.]"

Like many other soldiers, he preferred to refer his correspondents to the newspapers for account of battles, campaigns, and reviews. His urgent concerns were personal — how much money did they need at home, how could he get by until payday, what was the state of the farm, would his brothers enlist, where could he get a supply of stamps? In the first letter in this volume, he assured his parents, "anything from home is acceptable," and where letters from his family were concerned, he never changed his mind.

We owe a debt to Marcia M. Reid-Green, Henry Matrau's great-granddaughter, for making these letters available to all of us. She has not simply allowed them to be published by the University of Nebraska Press; she has also put in the time and labor to annotate them — no easy task. Publishing these letters is a way she can pay honor to her great-grandfather — but turning over an ancestor's words and memory to the world, particular to the devourous community of historians, must be a frightening thing to do. So I thank her for her industry, perseverance, and courage, the virtues she shares with Henry Matrau and the generation of Americans, North and South, black and white, men and women, who lived through our Civil War.

REID MITCHELL

Preface

WHEN I WAS a little girl in Denver, one of the delights of a rainy day was to go to the storeroom and pull open the old steamer trunk. There was my grandmother's leg-of-mutton-sleeved jacket and my mother's pink chiffon dress with rhinestones and ostrich feathers, a treasure from the flapper era. There, also, was a large manila envelope with the notation in my father's handwriting, "Grandfather Matrau's Letters." It was not until much later that I came to realize that this was the real treasure in the trunk, a complete set of copies of a young soldier's letters home throughout the Civil War. He had served with the famed Sixth Wisconsin, the Iron Brigade, from shortly after the start of the war until the general demobilization following Lee's surrender at Appomattox, seeing action at Second Bull Run, Fredericksburg, Gettysburg, the Wilderness campaign and the siege of Petersburg.

Many years later, my husband and I moved east with our son, Douglas. We made a family project of visiting the places Henry Matrau mentioned and Doug used the letters as the basis for school projects and reports. Inquiries to the remaining members of my father's family brought forth some additional information about Henry Matrau, especially from Bernice Ruddell, the great-granddaughter of Henry's brother Morgan. She sent her genealogy of the Matraus and some information about the Woodruffs, Henry's mother's family. No one, however, could shed light on what had become of the original letters or who had copied them so carefully. To that unknown typist must go my thanks as well as to Helen Zavitkovsky, my son's high school teacher, who became as interested in my great-grandfather as we are. She spent hours tracing his travels and delving into the idiomatic American language of the mid-1800s.

Through Helen, I became acquainted with Philip Crown of the Michigan Civil War Round Table. He has been an invaluable source of information and of suggestions for further research, having adopted Henry as the special focus of his interest in the war. Mrs. Crown, Tricia, also became involved as researcher and travel companion on repeated visits to the University of Michigan Library at Ann Arbor.

Later, Lance Herdegen of The Sixth Wisconsin Volunteers, North-South Skirmish Association, learned of the project. He sent excerpts from the association's newsletter, *The Black Hat*, and a copy of an article by Jerome Watrous, which he and William Beaudot were using for their own book, *In the Bloody Railroad Cut at Gettysburg*. Watrous was a veteran of the Sixth Wisconsin regiment and subsequently became editor of the *Milwaukee Sunday Telegraph*.

Mention must be made of the staffs of the Mercer County Library branches in Hopewell Township and Lawrenceville, New Jersey; the Maud Preston Palenske Memorial Library of St. Joseph, Michigan; the Berrien County Historical Association, especially Robert C. Myers, curator of the 1839 Courthouse Museum, Berrien Springs, Michigan; the office of the Berrien county clerk; the Norfolk, Nebraska, Chamber of Commerce; and the Visitors' Center of Petersburg, Virginia. Thanks are also due to my husband, Keith, the ever-patient computer maven and critic; and my son Douglas, the military historian and map consultant. Of course, the largest share of thanks belongs to Henry Matrau himself and to the family that never threw anything away.

Histories of the war and the brigade have been written many times, so my short chapter introductions are meant to provide a historical setting for the letters and to clarify references to events and people. A biographical list of friends, relatives, and officers mentioned in the letters may be found at the end of the book. Henry's original spelling, grammar, and punctuation have been altered slightly to improve clarity.

The Iron Brigade received its sobriquet at the Battle of South Mountain, September 14, 1862, when Major General Joseph Hooker, impressed by the steadiness and bravery of Gibbon's troops, referred to them as the "iron brigade" in reports to General McClellan. Gibbon's men proudly adopted the appellation, and that is how we now know them.

Chapter One

Letters of July 22, 1861, to February 27, 1862

HENRY CLAY MATRAU was born near Watervliet, Michigan, on April 2 or 24, 1845. (The family genealogy and a newspaper obituary give the earlier date, but Henry's Declaration for Pension, September 19, 1907, and an affidavit sworn by his sister, Lucy, on January 28, 1908, use the later one.[1]) The town is in Bainbridge Township, Berrien County, at the extreme southwest corner of the state, just across Lake Michigan from Wisconsin. Henry's paternal ancestors had come from France to a farm near Montreal, and subsequently his father, Joseph, moved south to the United States. At that time Joseph changed the spelling of the name from Metras to preserve the French pronunciation.

In 1835, Joseph was employed by a land-holding company, Smith and Merrick, in Niagara County, New York. After clearing timberland there during the winter, the work gang was ordered to move to Michigan. Several men refused to go so far west, but seventeen of them, including Joseph Matrau, walked to Buffalo, sailed across the lake to Detroit, and walked to Bainbridge. They spent the next twelve months clearing land and planting wheat and then moved on. When the contract expired, Smith and Merrick owed Joseph for his labor and by 1839 they still had not sent him the money. He returned to Bainbridge and took eighty acres in Section 28 as settlement of the debt. For three years, Joseph worked on the St. Joseph River while clearing his land. He was then able to farm full time, starting an apple orchard in 1843. Two of his brothers, Mitchell and Paul, also settled nearby, as did a nephew, MaGloire, who went by the name of Merritt.[2]

In 1842, Joseph married Amanda Woodruff, the daughter of Deacon Levi Woodruff, a pioneer who had settled in Bainbridge several years earlier. Levi was from New England but had moved to Broome County, New York, in 1806. He continued west in 1837 with his second wife and their four children, as well as six from his first marriage, including Amanda. The family settled on 160 acres purchased from Smith and Merrick, living first in an abandoned log cabin until their own house was completed. Levi was instrumental in the organization of a Congregational church in Bainbridge and served as a town supervisor in 1840. The road running by their home was named Deacon Street in his honor.[3]

Over the years, both the Matrau and the Woodruff families were active in township affairs, holding various offices in civic and religious organizations. Their names appear as members of the township board, clerk, treasurer, justice of the peace, supervisor, school inspector, members of the Grange, and on lists of church officers in the Congregational and Methodist Episcopal churches.[4]

At first, Joseph and Amanda lived a rugged frontier existence, relying on game to supplement their farm production and cooking by the fireplace. Amanda did her own spinning, weaving, and sewing. Once she tried to improve Joseph's scanty formal education, but he told her he could count money and that was sufficient. She continued in her family's religion, but

Joseph became affiliated with the Methodist Episcopal church, having abandoned his parents' Roman Catholic faith.[5] Their family eventually expanded to include six children, all of whom are mentioned in Henry's letters: Henry, born in 1845; Morgan W., born 1847; Benjamin Franklin (Frank), 1849; Levi W., 1855; Lucy L., 1857; and Edward N., 1860.

In 1850, the Matrau family moved to a farm in Section 14 of Bainbridge Township and consequently the children would have attended Bainbridge School in District 7, probably a one-room schoolhouse. In addition to the three R's, rural school teachers presented their students with a more extensive education than is generally realized, including geography, history, science and Latin.[6]

Henry grew up to be a sturdy, healthy boy whose round face made him appear younger than his years. By his sixteenth birthday, in 1861, he stood only five feet four and one-half inches tall. In spite of his short stature, Henry was determined to answer President Lincoln's call for volunteers following the attack on Fort Sumter, April 12, 1861. The local officials in Michigan declined to enroll him, so in May, Henry went to Chicago to try again. After two failures and the threat of arrest when he told a recruiting officer he "didn't know his business," he heard that a few places were open in a company being formed at Beloit, Wisconsin. He traveled to that city on July 11 and was accepted for state service as a private in Company G, the Beloit Star Rifles, representing Rock County. The captain cautioned that he might still be rejected by the federal army but Henry refused the suggestion that he play the fife or drum.[7]

From Beloit, the recruits were sent to Madison, Wisconsin, and were assigned to newly established Camp Randall, named for the governor, Alexander W. Randall, and situated on the

State Agricultural Society's fairgrounds. Its thirty acres included a frame headquarters building, commissary, hospital, stables, and whitewashed barracks accommodating one hundred men in three tiers of bunks. Meals were served at tables in the center aisles. Still more men were housed in tents; one captain, two lieutenants, or six men in each. The heart of the complex was the parade ground, and it was here on July 16, that the recruits were mustered into the U.S. Army for three years' service as one of ten companies in the Sixth Wisconsin Volunteer Regiment.[8] According to Jerome Watrous, a veteran of the regiment, Henry stuffed insoles into a pair of extra-large shoes with thick soles and heels and wore a high-crowned cap in order to pass the inspection of the mustering officer.[9] His first surviving letter home was written the following week.

Initial training was conducted at Camp Randall by Colonel Lysander Cutler, the Sixth Wisconsin's first commander. It was during this period, while the volunteers were parading in Madison, that Henry received his nickname. As Company G was passing, an onlooker spotted him and said, "Look at that little fellow, he's only a baby!" and the "Baby of Company G" he became. Nevertheless, according to Watrous, no other member of the regiment could load or fire more rapidly or keep up better on the march.[10]

On July 20, the First Battle of Bull Run was fought at Manassas Junction, Virginia. Confederate General P. G. T. Beauregard defeated Union General Irvin McDowell in full view of newspaper reporters and congressmen who had driven out from Washington to see the first major contest in the East. McDowell was promptly replaced as field commander by General George B. McClellan and talk of a ninety-day war ceased.[11]

In spite of a lack of arms — only two companies had been supplied — the Wisconsin regiments were ordered to Washington in late July and traveled there by train. At Baltimore, where many citizens were Southern sympathizers, the unarmed men had a police escort as they marched through town because the Sixth Massachusetts had been attacked by a mob several weeks earlier. On the night of August 5, they too were set upon while camped at Patterson Park and forced to defend themselves by throwing bricks. Subsequently, they were issued Belgian muskets, old weapons with a dreadful recoil that at least offered the guards a defense against "Secesher" attacks.[12]

It was not until the following February that the Wisconsin men finally received new American-made Springfields,[13] rifled muzzle-loading muskets that made formidable weapons when teamed with Minie bullets. They could kill at a half mile but were not accurate at that distance. Minie bullets were invented by a French officer in 1848; conical in shape, they made infantry fire about twice as effective as round shot. The soldiers called them "Minnies."[14]

After several days in Baltimore, the Wisconsin soldiers rode to Washington in filthy cattle cars, washed at fire hydrants, and marched to Camp Kalorama on Meridian Hill. On August 23 they were reviewed by Brigadier General Rufus King, whose command now consisted of the Fifth and Sixth Wisconsin and the Nineteenth Indiana. Four days later, the Second Wisconsin transferred to the brigade, having seen duty at Bull Run under Colonel W. T. Sherman. The group remained stable until October, when the Fifth Wisconsin was detached and the Seventh added. Governor Randall had hoped for an all-Wisconsin brigade, but the decision to retain the Nineteenth Indiana thwarted his dream. Nevertheless, General King's was the only completely western brigade in the Army of the Potomac.[15]

Most of the recruits in the brigade were from farms or small towns in what we today call the upper Midwest. Slightly over half were native-born American; the rest were German, Irish, Scandinavian, English, and Canadian.[16] Camp activities were accompanied by the sound of drums beating commands from sunup to night. The welcome last call of the day was tapped out by a lone drummer, hence the name "Taps" for what became the nightly bugle call.[17]

The Sixth Wisconsin left Camp Kalorama September 2 and moved to Camp Lyon on the Maryland side of the Chain Bridge, six miles above Washington. They spent the month on picket duty, a vitally important function since the opposing armies were located so close to each other. On October 15, the Army of the Potomac was organized into divisions and General King's brigade was assigned to General Irvin McDowell's division. The scattered regiments reunited at Fort Cass, on Arlington Heights, Virginia, not far from the home of Robert E. Lee, where the National Cemetery is now located.[18]

Also of importance in October was the arrival of Battery B of the Fourth U.S. Artillery, under the command of Captain John Gibbon. It was assigned to McDowell's division and promptly recruited volunteers from the infantry to fill its depleted complement. The presence of this professional military unit was a positive and steadying influence on the young volunteer soldiers.[19]

* * *

Camp Randall, Madison, Wis July 22/1861

Dear Parents,

I received your letter of the 15th last Saturday and was very glad to get a letter from home.

Smith [Young][a] got a letter from Wat[b] the same day. I got the letter Jo wrote but hav'nt had time to answer it. We are all well and in good spirits. We were mustered into the U.S. Service last Tuesday.

We got our uniform the day after. Our uniform is all grey. We have roundabout coats[c] and loose pants. It is the best fighting rig imaginable.[d] We received orders to day from Gen. Scott to proceed to Washington as soon as we [can] possibly get ready. We expect to go inside of three weeks.

Our knapsacks, haversacks, canteens, lint,[e] tents and everything but guns are here now. We have old U.S. muskets to drill with. Our gun will be the Enfield Rifle. It is the 6th Regiment to which I belong. The 5th is in camp with us. The ladies of Madison presented both regiments with a splendid banner each. The cost of each flag is estimated to be 100 dollars.

Afternoon — A telegraphic dispatch has just arrived giving accounts of a great battle in which the federals suffered [a] complete rout. Of the New York Zouave's 200 only escaped. Another ordering the 6th on to Washington next Monday. The 5th goes next Thursday. Our arms & equipments arrived this afternoon. The camp is all excitment. Hurrah's are heard all over. No more furloughs granted. We are to be paid next Wednesday.

Evening — The cooks of which there are 150 will be busy all night cooking provisions for our journey. Purfield[f] wants to have you write all the news in your next letter. He sends his best respects to you and all enquiring friends. We are living in tents now. There is a regular city of cloth tenements.[g] We have had a good deal of rain but our tents shed the rain as good as shingle roofs. Last week the ladies of Madison gave us a hansome supper. There were, it is estimated, 10,000 people on the camp ground. In the evening we had a dance on the green in which over 500 couple[s] participated. The dance lasted till 11 o'clock.

Tell the boys I will write to all of them when I can get time. We have to get up at 5 o'clock, drill till breakfast, which is at 7, then from 10 till 11, from 1 till 2, from 3 till 5; we don't get to bed till 10 o'clock so you see I havn't much time to write. Smith is as tough as a boiled owl and now with the rest of the boys hurahing for Richmond.

I must draw this to a close. Please write soon for anything from home is acceptable.

Your Son, Henry.

a. Henry's friend Smith Young enrolled in the army July 15, 1861, at the age of twenty-three. He mustered into the service as a private July 16 at Camp Randall.

b. Waterman Young, Smith's brother

c. Close-fitting jacket with no tails or skirt

d. At first, the states outfitted the men, although some individual units were raised, uniformed, and equipped by their own officers. The Wisconsin volunteers began the war in gray, as did several other Union regiments. See Alan T. Nolan, *The Iron Brigade*, 3d ed. (Berrien Springs, Mich.: Hardscrabble Books, 1983), 14; and John Selby, *The Iron Brigade* (New York: Hippocrene Books, 1973), 37, plate A. In September, these uniforms were replaced by the blue of the federal army, thus eliminating the confusion that was reported in early encounters such as the First Battle of Bull Run (see Morison, 628). Many of the volunteers felt the quality of the new uniforms was inferior to their state-issued grays and kept their original overcoats in spite of orders to the contrary (Nolan, 34).

e. A soft cloth used for a surgical dressing

f. Henry L. Purfield enrolled in the army July 15, 1861, at Beloit at the age of twenty-eight. He was mustered into service, along with Henry Matrau and Smith Young, as a private on July 16 at Camp Randall.

g. The word *tenements* means housing that is not occupied by the owner. It does not necessarily connote a slum.

Harrisburg Pa Aug 1st/61

Dear Parents,

We struck our tents here near the suburbs of the city yesterday in an oatfield. We had a very fine journey. We left Madison last Sunday morning & got to Milwaukee the same day at noon. There the citizens had a splendid dinner provided for us to which we did ample justice. At Chicago we had sandwiches, coffee, apples, & cigars passed around in the cars. At Ft. Wayne they didnt treat us quite as well. At every place we stopped the people came out in great numbers, cheered, and shook hands with us and at most places they filled our canteens with water and some with hot coffee. We got into Pittsburg Tuesday morning. The people of that smoky town turned out in great numbers & hot coffee and cakes were passed around in great abundance. Old Mitchel's Geography[a] told the truth when it said that Pittsburg was remarkable for its smoke.

Even the little newsboys running around the streets look as if they had [been] suspended over the funnel of some blacksmith's shop. You can smell smoke, feel smoke, & I will go so far as to say you can taste it.

Our route lay through the Alleghany Mountains & I had a chance of seeing some pretty tall hills. We went through three tunnels, one of which is a mile in length.

We are going to start for Harpers ferry tomorrow at 3 oclock in the afternoon. I have seen several of the soldiers who were in the battle of bulls run, they say the loss was full as great as was represented on our side but the Rebels lost a great many men too. They say that the southerners fight like tigers and are armed to the teeth. I had the honor of shaking [hands] with Major Anderson's daughter[b] at a small station on the top of the Alleghanys.

At one place the ladies threw Bouquets into the cars. Smith and Purfield are both well [and] in good spirits.

You hadn't better write till you hear from me again for I presume I should'nt get it. Give my love to all enquiring, reserving a large share for yourselves.

Your Affct Son, H. C. Matrau

a. Samuel A. Mitchell was the author of several travelers' guides, atlases, and geography books published in Philadelphia.
b. The daughter of Major (later General) Robert Anderson, who was in command of the Union troops at Fort Sumter

Baltimore Md. July [August] 4th/61

Dear Parents,

We arrived here last night & camped on the ruins of an old breastwork.

From our camp we can overlook the whole city. We are in full sight of Ft McHenry & can hear ocasionally the booming of guns as some war vessel salutes it in passing. We were cheered all along the road by the people as we passed.

We got a good many cheers as we passed through the city & I observed we got a good many curses as loyal as people may imagine the Baltimoreans to be. Our camp is called Patterson Park from an old revolutionary story connected with it. Gen. Patterson was camped here on the very place our tents are now pitched. He heard that a large British force was marching to attack him & he threw up the breastwork, the ruins of which now are to be seen. As Gen. Howe, the British commander, got in sight of Patterson's fortifications he drew his men up in a line

& pointing towards the American lines said: we will go into that town before tomorrow morning or I will go to hell.

A battle ensued in which he was defeated. There is a police [force] of 500 stationed here now. This place has the reputation of being the most riotous town in the union. A riot happened, I was told by a policeman, only a few days [ago] in which several were killed. We hav'nt got our arms yet but Im told they are in town waiting for us. We are to have the Minie musket. Our probable destination will be Harper's Ferry. We have had miserable fare & been used pretty rough scince we left Madison but now we are going to have our regular rations, which will be much better. I have seen some of the young city chaps who enlisted sick enough of the job. They find that the life of a soldier is'nt all pleasure after all. I never felt tougher or more rugged in my life. I find that the climate is much warmer here than in Wiscon. or Michigan; still the heat doesnt bother me a great deal.

Our 2nd Lieut [W. W. Allen] died this morning. He had been sick for 3 or 4 weeks but none of us expected he would die so sudden. Some think he was poisoned. Orders have been given us not to purchase anything to eat or drink at all under penalty of being bucked and gagged.[a]

Purfield & Smith are both well. Please write soon.

Your affct Son, H. C. Matrau

P.S. Direct to the 6th Wis Regiment
Company G. Baltimore Md.

a. *Bucking and gagging* was a punishment used in the field during the Revolutionary and Civil wars. It consisted of seating the offender on the ground with his knees drawn up to his chest. A stick was passed under the knees and the arms were placed under the stick. The hands were then tied in front of the legs. To prevent crying out during the punishment, a tent pin or bayonet was inserted in the mouth and tied in place.

Camp Kalorama Aug 15/61

Dear Parents:

Everything we see or hear in this place is the roll of the drum or the command "fall in" which in the course of 3 or 4 months hearing it becomes very dull amusement. We are situated on a rising swell of ground from which we can see the Potomac river & a part of Georgetown. The hills around here are mostly covered over with a thick growth of small timber; beech, maple, & oak. We don't know when we will pack up & leave here. We may stay a month & we may leave the next hour, it is uncertain. Gen. Scott is getting an immense force around the Capital which he will most likely keep till cooler weather when he will make a demonstration the rebels little expected. The New York 69th Reg. stationed nearer the city revolted a day or two ago and killed two of their officers. The revolt was occasioned by refusing to allow them to go home after their time was out. The revolt was quelled upon their being allowed the privilege of going home.[a] A soldier is not supposed to know anything outside of his own camp. When we are ordered to sling knapsacks & prepare for march we don't know what it is for or where we are going. Tell the boys if they want to be free & not be obliged to come & go at the beck of an officer to stay at home & leave sogering to those that like it. A person in the army must mind his own business & let other people's alone or it will be apt to go pretty hard with him.

There is one of our company obliged to stand guard a week for not being prompt to obey orders & for getting asleep on his post. Standing guard here is different from standing guard in Michigan. One is apt to here the sharp zip of the bullet as he treads his beat. One night while we were in Baltimore there were as many as 30 shots fired at the guard but fortunately but one shot took effect & that broke the leg of a secesher.

There are two Massachusetts Regiments near us & all composed of solid and intelligent men. They were out on parade yesterday & presented a very fine appearance.

The Michigan boys are all well but Geo Jay & C Gibbs, who are down with the summer complaint.[b]

16th morning:

Last night one of our guard deserted his post, it is believed for the enemy. Heavy firing was heard about two miles distant from here. Our Regiment is in good spirits & confident that it won't be long before we have a chance at them.

Yours, Henry

a. The original call for volunteers carried a three-month term of enlistment. Subsequently, longer periods were established. Henry and his friends enlisted for three years.

b. The weather was very hot, the water bad, and many men suffered from "summer complaint," a severe diarrhea brought on by bacterial contamination of food and water. It was prevalent throughout the war as a consequence of poor sanitation practices and led to many deaths in both Northern and Southern camps, hospitals, and prisons.

During the four years of the war, sudden and uncontrolled attacks of infectious diseases such as typhoid, typhus, malaria and other fevers, diarrhea, dysentery, tuberculosis, measles, and smallpox resulted in far more casualties than did battle wounds. Records are incomplete, especially for the Confederacy, but in 1865, the adjutant general's office published the following figures:

Union admissions to sick report, 5,825,480, of which almost 1,400,000 were diarrhea.

Combined Union and Confederate battle deaths, 204,070

Combined Union and Confederate deaths due to disease, 388,586

The usual treatments consisted of dosing with oil of turpentine, ipecac, or quinine, when supplies were available. Preventive measures were seldom taken and disease became a factor in the outcome of many battles. See Paul E. Steiner, *Medicine of the Civil War* (Washington, D.C.: The National Library of Medicine, n.d.), 3, 8.

Camp Lyon Sept 17th

Dear Parents,

I received yours and Ange's[a] letters about 2 weeks ago but we have been moveing around so much that I have'nt had time to write.

We left Camp Kalorama two weeks ago & marched up the river about 5 miles & camped near the chain bridge in an apple orchard. We marched across the river last Wednesday to fight the rebels who were advancing in a large body on to our lines but though we marched double quick to the scene of action we came too late, the rebels had retreated taking with them their dead and wounded.

There were 6 killed & 2 or 3 wounded on our side. The loss of the Confederates is not known but is supposed to be considerable. Purfield, Smith & the rest of the Michiganders are all well. I have sent by express ten $10 dollars to father in the care of B. C. Hoyt, St. Joseph, which will be mailed the same day as this.[b] Smith will fill up the sheet to his folks & you can show them this letter. I can't write any more at present. Please write soon.

Your affectionate Son, H. C. Matrau

[In a different hand]   Camp Lyons Sept the 17th 1861

Pow [Paw?] Som [Sam?] I will rit a fiew lines to you to let you no that I am right side up with Care every time hank has told you the nuse Som I cent 15 dolars to you Directed to father in care of B C Hoyt St Joseph and if you get it let me now for if you dont I dont blieve I will send eney more and hank wanted his folks to do the same

Smith Young

[In the first hand]
P.S. You can get the gold on the treasury notes at any bank. You had better get the gold for them as soon as possible for Uncle Sam may issue more paper than he can redeem.[c]

H. C. Matrau

a. Angeline, Henry's cousin

b. In the letters, Henry repeatedly reports sending money home in care of B. C. Hoyt, a banker at St. Joseph, Michigan, the county seat of Berrien County.

c. Before the end of 1861, the U.S. Treasury did indeed discontinue the redemption of Treasury notes in gold or silver. "Greenbacks," officially known as Demand Notes, were issued with no metal reserve. This paper money fluctuated in value but was legal tender and had to be accepted as such. See Christopher C. Chamberlain and Fred Reinfeld, *Coin Dictionary Guide* (New York: Sterling Publishing Co., 1960), 177–78. As the war progressed, paydays were very irregular, causing Henry problems, but he continued to send money to the bank rather than keep it on his person.

Ft Cass Oct 7th

Dear Parents,

I wrote a letter & Smith wrote a line on the space that was left at the same time we sent the money home. Smith sent $15.00 and I sent $10.00. We both sent our money by express in care of B. C. Hoyt. Smith has got a letter from home stating they had got the money Smith sent. I should have had an answer the same time Smith did, I suppose, if the mail did its business up brown. But as it is I did'nt get any answer as to whether the money was received or not. I am well; so is Smith & the rest of the Mich[igan] boys. We moved from our old camp near the chain bridge to Ft Cass at Arlington heights on the sacred soil of Virginia. We expect to be ordered on to Richmond in a little while. Gen. Scott intends to make some grand movement before winter sets in. We are 3 miles from Munsons hill which was lately occupied by the Rebels until our men drove them off.

The 7th Wis. Reg't is camped right by our side. They are in the same Brigade we are in. Gen. King is Brigadier Gen. The most of the Brigade is together now. We are on top of a hill nearly surrounded by trees. From the tops of some of the trees we can see the work of our soldiers for miles. The trees are all chopped down clear to the Potomac. I can't think of any thing more to write. Please write as soon as you get this, for you can't think how I like to get letters from home. Give my love to all enquiring friends, reserving a large share for yourselves and family. Kiss Levi, Lucy, and the baby [Edward] for me. Please pardon all mistakes, for I had a bad pen & a hard place to write on.

From your Affectionate Son, H. C. Matrau

P S Tell John Worden[a] I will answer his letter as quick as possible but I don't know how quick it will be, we have so much to do & we don't know when [we] shall have to move.

a. The Wordens were members of the Methodist Episcopal church, as was Joseph Matrau.

Arlington Heights Nov 20/61

Mr Matrau.

Dear Sir.

I take this opportunity to write a few lines to let you know how I prosper & how we soldier boys average. Us Mich[igan] chaps are all well & stand sogering better than most of the Wisconsin plugs do.

Henry is as tough & hearty as a young buck deer & does duty & stands his guard with the rest of them. We all expect to be at home ere the Ides of March make their appearance. It is so cold here now that still water freezes in the night to the depth of a quarter of an inch. We all have fire places in our tents of our own manufacture & invention. So you see we manage to keep warm in our tents. Standing guard is'nt quite so funny. But we manage to keep warm marching double quick up & down our beats. We are better clothed than any other Regiment in the Service. Our Regiment was paid off yesterday our regular 26 dollars apiece. You will find enclosed a little breast pin with the likeness of Gen McClellan photographed which is for little Lucy also a photograph likness of Col. Ellsworth,[a] which is for Mrs Matrau. I must bring this to a close. Please write soon

Your Friend H. L. Purfield

a. Elmer E. Ellsworth, a Union hero early in the war

Arlington Heights Va Jun [Jan] 11th/62[a]

Dear Parents,

I received your kind letter yesterday and was very glad to get news from home once more. We Michigan chaps are all well at present and in good spirits, though the weather at present is rather unfavorable to an exuberance of good feeling, especially for men who "keep house" in such frail tenements as we soger's have to put up with. It has been wet, disagreeable weather for the past week and the way the "sacred soil of Virginny" sticks to the boots of the humble pedestrian is a caution to Davy Crockett. The other morning while going down to the messroom I lost both shoes in the mud and had to call out a corps of Sappers and miners to get them out. Perhaps you will feel inclined to disbelieve this story but I tell it merely to put emphasis on the assertion. We were on picket the other side of Fall's Church last week but didn't meet with any remarkable adventures other than the capture of 4 Contrabands,[b] who we delivered up to Uncle Sam, their rightful owner.

It is very dull here now and we are all anxious to make a forward movement. But I suppose it will be 2 or 3 months before there will be any chance for a scrummage.

I have seen Gen. McClellan a good many times and have been to more than one review at which he commanded in person. It was through the influence of Gen. McClellan that our regiment got the best arms in the service. When you write please tell me how to direct a letter to Angeline and I will write to her. I would also write Uncle Philo[c] a letter if I knew his address.

Please write often: Give my love to the children.

From your Affct Son, H. C. Matrau

a. The dateline on this letter is puzzling, since the Sixth Wisconsin was at Falmouth opposite Fredericksburg in June, 1862. External evidence indicates that the correct month is January, when the regiment was at Arlington Heights.

b. The word *contraband* usually refers to smuggling, but during the Civil War it referred to Negro slaves who escaped to or were brought within Union lines.

c. Amanda's brother, who had moved to Minnesota in 1856

Arlington Heights Va. Jan 31st/62

Dear Parents,

I take this opportunity to write you a few lines to let you know I am still alive and well and hope these few lines will find you enjoying the same. The weather still continues to be wet and disagreeable, the mud is knee deep and adown every hill torrents of clayey mud and water are running down filling up the little hollows and creeks with which eastern Virginia abounds. It is so muddy that we have nothing to do but get our fire wood to keep our little fire places agoing.

Once in every 22 days we have to go out and do 3 or 4 days picket duty but this don't bother us much. We have got side walks laid down corduroy fashion all over the camp so our camp has some the appearance of a well regulated village.

Our large family get along quite peaceably together and only occassionly a fist fight serves to break the monotony of camp life. There are only 20 prisoners in the guard house and they are all soldiers.

Some are in for disobeying officers, some for getting intoxicated, some for running the guard, and some for stealing.

While I am writing there are a couple of fellows pacing up and down in front of the guard house with a barrel thrust over each one's head for stealing. Smith wanted me to ask you to inquire of Mr Young if he got the money he sent him. It was 15 dollars. I would have sent 15 or 20 dollars home had I not the good luck to lose my wallet with 24 dollars in it while I was out on picket. Inclosed you will find the picture of our old Colonel [Lysander Cutler] one of best old chaps that ever said "right face" or "forward march." I can't think of any more to write at present. Please write often.

Your Aff'nt Son, H. C. Matrau

Arlington Heights Va Feb 27th/62

Dear Parents,

I take this opportunity to write you a few lines to let you know I'm still alive and well. We are still at our old camp on the Heights but expect to leave it soon. We have just had orders to throw away all the clothing we do not actually need and hold ourselves in readiness to start at a moments notice. We have had our cartridge boxes filled with new and good cartridges and new canteens & haversacks given out to us, in short, everything needed for a long tramp. When we leave here, we leave our tents also and every unnecessary baggage. Only four wagons will be allowed to a regiment. One of these will [be used] to carry ammunition and the rest our provision. When we start it is'nt likely that we'll stop far this side of Bull's Run, and McLellan will do his best to smoke out that nest of hornets. He will storm Manassas at the point of the bayonet. And to make us proficient in the art of punching our fellow man we have been for the last month drilling in the bayonet exercise.[a]

It is strange what a predeliction we have for injuring our brother man, but we learn the art of killing far easier than we do a hard problem in arithmetic. The sun is out shining brightly and the wind blowing a gale and the ground is drying off very fast.

All are anxious to move and the boys look smiling enough

when there is any chance for a scrummage. But I must bring this to a close. You must keep up as good a face as possible and a stiff upper lip for you'll see me at home in July.

From your Son, H. C. Matrau
"To the old folks at home".

a. While the Union soldiers spent the winter in target practice, drilling, and occasional picket duty, the Confederate Army of Northern Virginia was camped around Manassas, Leesburg, and Centerville. The War Office in Washington became increasingly impatient with McClellan's reluctance to attack, and finally, January 27, Lincoln issued an unprecedented order to his general to advance on February 22. Still, McClellan did not move until March.

Chapter Two

Letters of March 28, 1862, to September 27, 1862

GENERAL McCLELLAN's grand plan called for a flanking move on Richmond by water rather than a direct march overland from Washington. The federal government finally agreed but insisted that adequate troops be left to protect the capital from Confederate attack. In March, the president organized the Army of the Potomac into corps, placing the three divisions of I Corps under the command of General McDowell. Rufus King was promoted to the resulting vacant division command and Lysander Cutler took over the brigade temporarily.[1]

Just as this announcement was made, McClellan learned that the Confederate Army was withdrawing from northern Virginia and hurried his troops to Centerville, Manassas, and Leesburg. There he found much weaker defenses than reports had led him to believe. In fact, the Southerners left behind "Quaker" guns, logs painted to resemble cannon. Cutler's brigade took part in this foray, their first action of the new year, but soon found themselves back in their old camp. They were further disappointed when McDowell's corps was detached from the Army of the Potomac and did not embark at Alexandria with the other troops. Two divisions did eventually join McClellan, but King's men took no part in the Peninsular campaign. McDowell's forces became the Department of the Rappahannock and reported directly to the War Department, as did the others retained in West Virginia and the Shenandoah. McClellan was no longer the general-in-chief.[2]

In April, McDowell moved south from Alexandria toward what was to be his new headquarters in Fredericksburg. Cutler's brigade, marching past Manassas, had to contend with snow, rain, and mud but eventually reached Catlett's Station, where they spent a week repairing the Orange and Alexandria Railroad. They then advanced to Falmouth, directly across the river from Fredericksburg. Here they turned to civil engineering, helping to repair two bridges the Confederate Army had destroyed when retreating from Virginia. On April 30, McDowell officially occupied the city.[3]

The following week, Cutler relinquished temporary command of the brigade and returned to the Sixth Wisconsin. The new leader was John Gibbon of Battery B, recently named brigadier general of volunteers. As a regular army man, Gibbon would not tolerate sloppy appearance or performance, but he was fair and instituted a system of rewards as well as punishments. He drilled the men hard, believing it his job to turn good volunteers into first-class soldiers. Finally, he ordered the men to wear new uniforms, largely regular army blue but with white leggings and gloves and a black felt hat with a large plume on the side that soon gave the men their first nickname, the Black Hat Brigade. It was the regular army's Hardee dress hat, introduced in 1855 and named for Captain William J. Hardee, the author of *Hardee's Tactics*.[4] All in all, it is Gibbon to whom credit is due for the emergence of the brigade as a distinctive fighting unit.

In late May, just as McDowell was starting a move toward Richmond in support of McClellan's Peninsular campaign,

Stonewall Jackson attacked the Union forces at Front Royal, Virginia. Lincoln ordered McDowell to halt and detach part of his command to the Shenandoah Valley. King's division turned around and through forced marches in hot, muggy weather arrived at Catlett's Station on May 31. Some of the men immediately boarded trains but the rest had to wait for more cars to arrive. Meanwhile, Jackson retreated, having achieved his goal of halting McDowell's advance, so all of King's men were eventually ordered back to Falmouth. The enlisted men blamed McDowell for these confused and futile moves, whereas the officers tended to criticize the civilians in Washington for trying to direct an army in the field.[5]

To bring order to the confused command, Lincoln brought John Pope east from Tennessee and appointed him general of the Army of Virginia on June 26. The various divisions scattered around Washington and northern Virginia were organized into new corps, with McDowell's as III Corps, and Pope moved to concentrate them along the line of the Rappahannock.[6]

Also in late June, McClellan's men suffered their first serious setback outside of Richmond and were forced to retreat across the peninsula. This movement placed Lee's Confederates between them and Pope's army. General King's cavalry units at Fredericksburg were therefore busy all of July scouting for enemy advances north. For Gibbon's infantry, however, it was back to drilling and discipline to eliminate weak spots he had noticed during the past few weeks.[7]

On July 23, Henry Halleck, the new general-in-chief, arrived in Washington. The first week of August he ordered McClellan to evacuate the peninsula. Pope was therefore directed to increase his efforts against Confederate communications and prevent a buildup of forces opposing McClellan's movements. The infantry joined the cavalry in raids against Southern railroads and telegraph wires, and Gibbon's men saw hard marching and some skirmishes with the enemy. The Sixth Wisconsin, charged with protecting a bridge needed for retreat at the end of the mission, missed the actual fighting.

At the same time, Pope started to advance his army to threaten a Confederate concentration southwest of Fredericksburg. Lee decided that McClellan was indeed leaving the peninsula and moved to attack Pope in his exposed position, thus reversing roles. On August 18, Pope realized his danger and ordered a retreat back to the Rappahannock. He held the north bank several days under heavy cannon fire, until reinforcements from McClellan arrived. Lee then sent Jackson around the Union right. Pope thought he was headed for the Shenandoah, but instead Jackson swung north to Manassas, capturing that Northern supply base and cutting the railroad line. Belatedly, Pope started to move north.[8]

On August 28, General King's division, including the Black Hat Brigade, set out on the Warrenton Turnpike, marching with intervals between brigades. No immediate danger was anticipated, so it was a complete surprise when Gibbon's men came under fire from Stonewall Jackson's artillery near Brawner Farm outside of Gainesville. Jackson, who had been hiding until Lee could join him, had just been notified that reinforcements were nearby, so he was free to attack as he saw fit.

The battle developed with extremely heavy musket fire at about seventy-five-yard range for almost two hours. General Gibbon sent requests for aid to General King, but only two regiments were dispatched. There was very little movement for all the fierce fighting, and the battle ended at darkness with both sides withdrawing from the field. Among the casualties was Colonel Cutler, who was wounded in the leg.

An English observer noted, "The men who faced each other that August evening fought with a gallantry that has seldom been surpassed," and a Confederate observed that the "Black Hatted fellows" had taken a terrible toll. General Gibbon was quoted as saying that he was proud to be commanding the men whom he had called "green" just ten days before.[9]

General King and his staff decided to move toward Manassas Junction to find support rather than face Jackson the next day, and the men left the scene of their first real battle around midnight. It was daybreak when they reached their destination. Later, on the 29th, the brigade fell in behind General Porter's corps as Pope moved to overwhelm Jackson. Skirmishers had exchanged fire that morning and a battle had developed near Groveton, during which Longstreet arrived to reinforce Jackson. Late in the afternoon, Gibbon reached the scene of the Second Battle of Bull Run, but the brigade was detached to support the reserve artillery. That night they slept on the ground in full gear.[10]

The second day, the Black Hat Brigade moved into battle behind two others. When the leading units were repulsed and fell back in confusion, Gibbon ordered his men to stop the retreat with bayonets and gunfire if necessary. The broken brigade steadied, but the federal attack was defeated.[11] A Confederate counterattack was successful, and Pope ordered a general retreat with the Black Hat Brigade covering the rear.

The entire encounter was marked by confusion and delay in the execution of orders. When he reached Washington, General Pope was replaced by General McClellan, who also retained command of his Army of the Potomac.[12]

McClellan rearranged his combined forces, returning McDowell's corps to its original designation of I Corps. McDowell, however, was gone to face a court of inquiry and Hooker took his place. The I and IX corps were designated the Right Wing, with General Burnside as commander. Within Hooker's corps, King's division was named the First Division, but King was relieved by Hatch. Gibbon's Black Hat Brigade became the Fourth Brigade in Hatch's division.[13]

Meanwhile, General Lee had crossed the Potomac and entered Maryland. He hoped to induce the state to join the Confederacy (parts of Maryland were sympathetic to the South), recruit men, and obtain supplies. He also wanted to draw the Federal troops further north, away from Richmond. On September 6, the Army of the Potomac moved to follow, and a week later they marched through Frederick and crossed the Catoctin Mountains. Henry was not with them, having been left in Washington on sick call.

On the 14th, the Black Hat Brigade and Battery B were on the National Road nearing the center of the Confederate line at Turner's Gap through South Mountain, while other forces attacked the flanks. Under heavy fire, they advanced up the steep incline, driving the defenders back into the gorge. At the top of the pass, the battle reached its climax after darkness had fallen. Firing ceased about 9 PM and the Southerners retreated shortly thereafter. Gibbon's brigade suffered severe casualties, about 25 percent, more than any other federal brigade. Generals Burnside and McClellan had seen the entire battle and were lavish in their praise, and General Hooker referred to the men as his "Iron Brigade."[14] The term stuck, and the Black Hatted Fellows assumed a new name.

Lee now established a defensive position behind Antietam

Creek around the town of Sharpsburg. McClellan's forces arrived on September 16 but delayed for a day, thus giving time for Southern units to reinforce Lee. Still, when the Battle of Antietam started, the North outnumbered the South seventy-five thousand to fifty thousand.[15] It was as well for Henry that he was not with the brigade at this time, because the seesaw battle took a terrible toll, the heaviest for any single day of the war. The Iron Brigade counted 42 percent casualties, with the Sixth Wisconsin suffering the most; 152 of its 314 officers and men were killed or wounded.[16] They had moved out early in the morning under heavy artillery fire, driving Southern pickets from the Miller farm buildings and then advancing, some through the cornfield and some through the West Woods. Just as they reached the Dunker Church, reinforcements joined the Confederates and drove the Union men back. The lines surged back and forth in the corn. At one time, the enemy was within fifteen yards of the guns of Battery B. Finally, I Corps was withdrawn and midmorning found the Iron Brigade supporting heavy artillery at the rear of the action. Except for some minor activity, the battle was over for them. Toward nightfall, the Confederates stopped a Union thrust into Sharpsburg and the fighting finally ceased.

On the 18th, General McClellan refused to renew the battle, although he had fresh reserves available and Lee's army had been terribly weakened. That night, Lee and Jackson retreated back into Virginia. The immediate crisis had ended, but McClellan was severely criticized for his failure to pursue the Confederate Army.[17]

The federal army camped at Sharpsburg, reorganizing, resting, and adding reinforcements. On October 4, John Reynolds became the third commander of I Corps, replacing Hooker.

The new Twenty-fourth Michigan arrived on October 8 to bolster the Iron Brigade, which had by now lost 58 percent of its original strength.[18] During late September and October, a number of wounded and ill men also returned to service, including Henry.

* * *

Fairfax Seminary Va March 28/62

Dear Parents,

I take this opportunity, the first I've had for two weeks, of writing anything. For the last two weeks we have been on the tramp most of the time. March 7th we had orders to march on to Manassas. We started in the morning at 4 oclock and marched 20 miles, which took us within 5 miles of Bulls run where we halted and pitched our tents.

The rebels had heard of our movement and left the place as fast their legs would carry them toward Richmond. We staid there 4 days when our brigade was ordered to Alexandria to take steamers and go down the river to reinforce Gen. Burnside. We are now camped about a mile and a half from the City of Alexandria waiting for the steam transports that are to take us down the river. I am well, with the exception of a slight cold caused by getting wet and sleeping in the mud. There are 60,000 men camped within sight of my tent. I must bring this to a close. Please write soon.

From Your Soger Boy, H. C. Matrau

P.S. Tell Uncle Newton[a] I got a letter from him yesterday and will answer as soon as I can.

a. Amanda's brother, a resident of Bainbridge

Camp beyond Manassas Apr 10/62

Dear Parents,

I take this opportunity to write you a few lines to let you know I am alive and kicking. We are encamped 15 miles south of Manassas junction on a small creek that Mr. Whitaker[a] calls Hawkanauk river. Smith did'nt come with us. He was sick and staid behind at Alexandria.

On our march here we came in sight of Bull run battle field. there is a good many dead horses and once in a while the skeleton of a poor soldier who has laid his life down for the star-spangled banner may be seen scattered over the field. When we camped day before yesterday we had got pretty desperately hungry and the consequence was the confiscation of a good many pigs, poultry, sheep, calves, turkeys, &c, belonging to good loyal rebels. We charged into a drove of about 100 sheep and the balls whistled pretty smartly for a while. One poor devil of a soldier who was in for his share of the mutton had a nice big quid of tobacco knocked out of his left cheek by a spent musket ball. We are driving the rebels back as fast as legs can carry them. We had as heavy a snow storm all day yesterday and last night as I ever saw in Mich. in the month of March.

Our old Colonel Cutler has been promoted to the Command of the brigade. Gen. King the old com[mander] has been promoted to the command of McDowells Division. I got a letter from Frank [Henry's brother] about two weeks ago but we have been moving about so much I couldnt find time to answer it. I must bring this to a close. Please write soon.

From your Affct son, H. C. Matrau

a. The Reverend Alexander Whitaker published *Good News from Virginia* in the early 1600s. See James D. Hart, *The Oxford Companion* to *American Literature*, 4th ed. (New York: Oxford University Press, 1965), 913.

Camp opposite Fredericksburg Va

July 6th 62/

Dear Parents,

I got my profile taken yesterday[a] and take this opportunity to let you know I'm well and hope this will find you enjoying the same. This is the first time I've had my picture with my soldier's toggery on and I thought you would be curious to see how I looked. I had my cartridge box and haversack on. There is some talk of our leaving here before long for Richmond. They have sent the sick to Washington and also all the extra quartermaster's stuff.

The drum is beating for Sunday morning inspection and I must close.

Your Affectionate Son, Henry C. Matrau

a. Henry's "profile" (photograph) shows him wearing the new uniform provided by General Gibbon — a blue frock coat with light blue trim, light blue trousers and white leggings. (No black hat, however, but the standard kepi.)

Georgetown D. C. Sept 13th/62

Dear Parents,

I take this opportunity to write you a few lines to let you know that I am still alive and getting along as well as circumstances will allow. For the last month we have had rough times, I tell you. The Rebs threw bomb shells, railroad iron, horse shoes, wrought iron nails, and solid shot at our devoted persons for 2 consecutive weeks. We could'nt make a fire to boil a cup of coffee but what "fiz, bang!" an old shell or piece of railroad would come over in among us and spoil our breakfast for that time. It was curious to see what effect the first shells they threw at us had on our Reg't. We could hear the discharge of a rebel cannon a great way of[f]. A minute after, "whiz," an old shell would come right over our heads. Every head was down in an instant, till the missile struck the ground, when the heads were all up again and laughing at each other for dodgeing. The battle we had happened just about sundown near a small railroad Sta. called Gainesville. We were [moving] leisurely along the road towards manasas junction when the Reb's opened on us with a battery of field pieces. We planted a battery on a hill and shells were flying thick and fast. Of our brigade the 19th Ind., 7th & 2nd Wis. were ordered up to attack the rebel infantry who were suporting their battery & our reg't was ordered down the road to suport our battery. We formed a line behind our battery and laid down behind a fence in a ditch. The shells all went over us. We laid there 2 minutes when the musketry began. The Gen's aid[e] came up on a gallup and ordered us up to form on the right, the rebs were trying to flank us. We scrambled over the fence, wheeled up facing the rebs who were in a piece of woods, and let a heavy volley into them when each man loaded and fired as fast as he could for an hour and fifteen minutes. We drove the rebs off the field and retreated ourselves. We [had] 700 men killed and wounded out of our bragade, 3 killed and 6 wounded out of our company. The Rebels lost 2200 killed and wounded according to their own story. Two days after that we fought a battle on the old bull run battle ground and owing to bad generals were forced to retreat back across the potomac. Our Reg't is now way up in Fredericktown keeping Jackson from Baltimore. I was tired out and staid behind. I am getting rested and will catch up with the regt soon.

Write soon, H. C. Matrau

Camp near Sharpsburg M.D. Sept 27th/62

Dear Parents,

When I wrote you last I was in Georgetown. The next monday we got on the cars and came on to Frederick. From Frederick we came on to the Antietam battle field where we are now encamped. I was'nt in the battle myself but our old brigade was cut up very bad. There were 3 killed & 14 wounded out of our company alone & some other companies in the Reg't suffered worse than ours. Our Michigan squad suffered pretty severely. Smith was wounded in the side and Hiram Whitaker was killed. They were both working the guns in our battery. Burt Miller [who] was in battery was also wounded and John Lane was wounded in the leg. Smith's wound was a bad one but I think he will recover. There are but three left now of the 17 Michigan boys that enlisted in this company. I think the number has decreased rather fast.

I feel pretty well now and do duty in the company as usual. Every house in the country is full of wounded. They are being taken away as fast as possible. We dont know how soon we will leave here. We may leave here tomorrow and we may stay here a month. I must bring this to a close. Please write soon.

Your Aff'nt son, Henry Matrau

p.s. I couldnt get any ink so I was obliged to use a lead pencil.

Chapter Three

Letters of December 10, 1862, to April 3, 1863

IN LATE OCTOBER, the Army of the Potomac left Maryland and returned to Virginia. There, Brigadier General John Gibbon was promoted to commander of the Second Division of I Corps and Colonel Henry Morrow replaced him temporarily. When Colonel Cutler was able to return to duty in November, he took over as brigade commander.[1]

In another November change, General McClellan was replaced by Ambrose Burnside. The new commander retained the existing corps but organized them into three "Grand Divisions." John Reynolds's corps (I Corps) was one of two in the Left Division, commanded by General William Franklin. The corps consisted of three divisions, with Major General Abner Doubleday heading the one containing the Iron Brigade. In December, Solomon Meredith of the Nineteenth Indiana became a brigadier general and assumed permanent command of the brigade, while Lysander Cutler, temporarily commander of the brigade, returned to his regular position in the regiment.[2]

With the army reorganized and properly supplied, the new commander headed toward Richmond. He arrived at the Rappahannock in good time on November 17 but delayed crossing because bridge-building material was not yet available. Lee took advantage of the time to fortify the heights behind Fredericksburg on the south bank of the river and bring reinforcements from the Shenandoah Valley. When the federal troops finally did proceed on December 11 and 12, the river was rain swollen and fire from the Confederates was heavy. Once skirmishers secured footholds on the southern side, the main army advanced on pontoon bridges, Franklin's grand division crossing downriver from the town. On the 13th, the Iron Brigade was ordered to advance into Smithfield Wood against General "Jeb" Stuart and secure a defense line on Meade's flank (his division was next to Doubleday's.) They were successful and held the position for the rest of the day under heavy artillery fire.

Late in the afternoon, Doubleday ordered Meredith to strengthen his line by withdrawing to trenches, leaving pickets in front. Some confusion in the execution of orders led to Meredith's dismissal, although he was reinstated after the battle. Colonel Cutler took command of the brigade and the men settled in for a miserably cold night, disturbed by Rebel picket fire and canister from the big guns.[3]

The day had been worse for the rest of the army. At Fredericksburg, Burnside ordered a direct assault on Lee's forces entrenched behind the town. Charge after charge was sent up the hills, but the costly effort proved futile.[4]

All day December 14, Burnside occupied ground on the enemy's side of the river while deciding whether to renew the attack. On the 15th he ordered a withdrawal, and that evening the artillery crossed the river, followed by the infantry. The Nineteenth Indiana was on picket duty and Cutler refused to abandon them. They managed to reach the river just after the bridges were cut and cross in boats with the engineers. The two armies then retired to winter quarters, Lee having won the most lopsided victory of the war.

The Union camp was located about twelve miles from Fredericksburg near the town of Belle Plain at the confluence of the Potomac River and Potomac Creek.[5] Once again, the soldiers settled into a tent city and the routine of housekeeping chores, drill, and picket duty. Their food consisted of flour, rice, beans, salt pork, salt beef, sugar, coffee, molasses, and bread, usually hardtack. Herds of cattle were driven along with the troops where possible to provide some fresh, if tough, beef. Soldiers could sometimes supplement this diet by purchasing fresh produce from local farmers or by raids on the herds and goods of Southern sympathizers. The cooks were usually ordinary soldiers with no particular training or skill.[6]

In January, the routine of the camp was broken by "the march in the mud," an attempt by Burnside to accomplish another crossing of the Rappahannock. The weather was terrible, either heavy rain or drizzle, and the army literally became bogged down. They left camp on the 20th and by the 24th were back, in miserable condition. The losses to pneumonia and other maladies were as severe as the casualties in some regular battles. The desertion rate, already high, shot higher still.[7]

On January 25, General Hooker replaced General Burnside. He immediately took steps to improve the morale of the troops through better food and the introduction of corps badges throughout the army. The insignia of the First Division of the I Corps was a red circle, which the men of the Iron Brigade proudly attached to their hats.[8]

Once again there were changes in command as Doubleday left the division and was replaced by James Wadsworth. Cutler was promoted to brigadier general and given the Second Brigade, so Lieutenant Colonel Bragg assumed the colonelcy of the Sixth Wisconsin.[9]

As the weather improved, last-minute details were completed in preparation for breaking camp. Colonel Bragg returned the Sixth Wisconsin's bullet-riddled flag to the governor and received a new one in exchange. The men, rested and ready for the new year of campaigning, awaited orders.[10]

* * *

Camp near Fredricksburg Dec 10th

Dear Mother,

We have been marching to day & have just halted for an hour or so. The report is that we are going to advance across the Rappahanock to night & I will improve a few moments in writing a few lines to you. I am well and hearty as usual. I will send 20$ by the Indiana Chaplain, who is going to washington, if I can. He is going to day. You wanted to know [who] our comanders were. The left grand Division, to which I belong, is commanded by Gen. Franklin. Our Corps is commanded by Gen. Reynolds. Our Division, which consists of four brigades, is comanded by Gen. Doubleday, our brigade by Gen. Meridith, our regiment by Colonel S. Cutler, our company by Capt. P. W. Plummer.

We were paid off last sunday, we got 52$.

I will send the money in the care of B. C. Hoyt as heretofore. I must close. We expect to go into a fight soon. May God defend the right.

Your Affct Son, Henry C. Matrau

P.S. I have just sent 20$ by the Chaplain.

Camp near Belle plain., Dec 22d/62

Dear Mother,

Scince I wrote you last we have had a terrible battle and have been totally defeated and obliged to retreat back across the Rappahanock.

Thanks to a merciful providence, I have been through the fiery ordeal unhurt, while 5000 brave fellows lay mouldering on the banks of the Rappahanock. Who is to be blamed for this enormous sacrifice of human life I leave to a more competent judge than I am. Soldier's are all discouraged. We think that this war is never going to be ended by fighting for the North & the South are to[o] evenly matched. No troops ever fought better than did our's the other day at Fredericksburg, but to no avail. Every hilltop was a fort and every ditch and tree sheltered gray coats. We retreated across the river in the night, as still as mice. We are within 3 miles of Belleplain Landing, a small village on the Potomac river. The talk is we are going into winters quaters, at least I hope so, for we are all worn out and tired of bumming around. The paper's all say that the soldiers are aching to fight, but the papers are notorious liars. We were never so fast to have the war brought to a close. The day before we crossed the river I sent 20$ home by express, also a letter. I directed the money to the care of B. C. Hoyt, St Jo, as usual. The army here is well clothed & well fed. I am as tough as usual. I have heard one of our wounded boys say that Smith [is] in a hospital in Alexandria, doing well, but he doesnt write & I dont know where to direct a letter to him.

I must close. Please write soon and tell me all the news. I have received a letter from Aunt Sarah[a] also one from Eugene & will answer both as soon as possible.

Your Affn't Son, H. C. Matrau

We are in Meridiths brigade, Doubledays Division, Reynolds Corps, & the Left grand division comanded by Gen. Franklin.

a. Wife of Uncle Asaph, Amanda's half-brother

Camp near Belle Plain Va- Jan 14th/63.

Dear Mother,

I received your kind letter of the 4th inst [Jan] yesterday and was glad to hear that the folks at home were in good health and prosperous. I am still as hearty as usual and take whatever comes in good part, as every soldier should, for there is no use to a soldier to grumble or be discontented at what he cant help.

We have been camped here about 6 weeks and have got pretty good winter quaters up, so we are beginning to live quite comfortable. Three of us have, by digging about 4 feet into the ground and raising it 6 log's high, then using our shelter tent for roofing, made quite comfortable quarters. We have got a bunk made of poles covered with cedar boughs in the place of feathers, in one end. In the other a regular old fashioned fire place. Our cupboard comprises a shelf on which you can see a frying pan, plate of beans, tin coffee cups, sugar & coffee bags, knife, fork, & spoon, big chunk of mess pork pies, and tobacco, &c, &c. Of reading matter we have a very limited supply, it consisting generally of the Dayly Chronicle, Times, Tribune, & Herald, & the novels Handy Andy, Irish Dragoon, [and] Flying Dutchman, so you see the variety is not great, neither is the literature very select or moral. We poor forlorn isolated portion of mankind, when we get a book, dont stop to consider whether it is of a moral religious tone or whether it tends toward's vice & immorality, but if it makes time pass away it is all we ask and you cant think it strange neither.[a]

I am sorry I wrote anything about poor Smith. I am afraid it has given rise to false hopes of his recovery by his folks. In my letter I meant to convey the meaning that it was merely a hearsay, a flying report of one of the returned wounded from Alexandria, about Smith getting well. There is nothing positive about it, and I am afraid it is without any foundation whatever.[b] If he were he would most certainly write to his Captain for his descriptive list[c] but neither the capt. nor I have received a word from him yet. It is impossible for one of us to get furlough now or even a pass to stay away over night. I have filled one sheet & not quite finished yet. You ask me if I think McClellan was true to his country. I think he was a great general and good & true patriot, & that is the opinion of every man in the army. Men that fought under him on the peninsula at south Mountain & Antietam all have this opinion of McClellan. Tell brother Morgan if he will take the advice of his luckless soldier brother he will steer clear of the army and stay at home with mother for take my word for it, though I'll own it aint romantic, a good soldier cares more for a good meal than he does for all the glory he can put in [a] bushel basket. I had forgot to tell you that I was appointed corporal about three months ago for good conduct,[d] so I aint a very great reprobate after all. Frank wanted to know if we get sugar or not. We get 3 table spoonfuls per diem regular.

I got a package of papers the other [day] from Mrs Yund.[e] They were a long time coming through but they come very acceptable I tell you. Tell Mrs Yund I thank her much. I must close. Please write often. Give my respects to all enquiring friends.

Your Aff'n'te Son, Henry Matrau.

P.S. The stamps came through all right.

a. *Handy Andy* was a novel published in 1842 by the Irish writer Samuel Lover. *The Irish Dragoon* was one of many plays by the American writer William Boyle Bernard, who lived from 1807 to 1875. The Flying Dutchman was a phantom ship condemned to haunt the sea forever because of a murder committed on board. It was the basis for a novel, *The Phantom Ship*, by the English writer Captain Marryat. See Paul Harvey, ed., *The Oxford Companion to English Literature*, 4th ed. (Oxford: Oxford University Press, 1967), 306, 491–92; and Hart, 75.

b. Henry's injured friend entered the medical system fairly early in the war and his chance for survival was not good. After battles, men were sometimes left on the field for as long as two days before being carried to treatment centers. Hospitals were set up in public buildings, homes, and even stables and barns. As the war progressed, care of the wounded became better organized and by the time of Gettysburg in 1863, almost every Union division had its own hospital located near a source of water. After treatment, soldiers were transferred to general hospitals.

Surgery was primitive and dangerous. Surgeons were often overwhelmed by the number of patients and worked around the clock with little or no assistance. Anesthetics such as chloroform were usually available but proper aseptic procedure was unknown. Nearly all wounds became infected and many limbs were amputated in an attempt to stop the spread of infection. Analgesic drugs consisted of morphine, opium, and whiskey. The average Union mortality rates for gunshot wounds of the chest and abdomen were 62 and 87 percent respectively. In contrast, during World War II, only three percent of American wounded died. See Steiner, 2.

c. A soldier's service record

d. Henry was promoted to corporal in November, 1862. (Pension and Military Records of Henry C. Matrau. General Reference Branch, National Archives and Record Service (NARS), Washington, D.C.)

e. The Yunds were neighbors who owned a farm near the Matrau home.

Camp near Belle Plain Va., Feb 9th/63

Dear Mother,

I received your kind letter of the 25th ultimo [Jan] & was glad to hear that the folks at home were enjoying good health and prosperous, I am as well as usual & thanks to an overruling Providence am permitted to enjoy our winter quarters, as yet. Burnside's army did'nt cross the Rappahannock, as I suppose you have heard ere this, although we made the attempt, got stuck in the mud & were obliged to wend our way with "mournful steps and slow" back to our old quarters. We have had two quite severe snowstorms here scince I wrote you last, although the weather is warm and pleasant now & has been for 3 or 4 days. We get hard crackers or rather pilot bread as it is called. I dont know whether you ever saw any or not so I'll tell you what kind of stuff it is.

It is made about the same size as common soda crackers we buy at home and prehaps a little thicker and made of two ingredient's only, viz. flour & water without salt, Saleratus,[a] or shortening, & baked as hard as a hot oven will bake them so you can imagine what kind of bread it is. We have lived on this kind of bread for over 8 months now. In order to make it more palatable we sometimes soak the crackers in water till they are soft, then fry them in salt pork grease.

Coffee is our perpetual beverage, coffee for breakfast, dinner, & supper. Tea is an article we can't get although we hanker after it more prehaps than anything else. Whiskey is scarce & sold only to officers, so intemperance is an evil we are not liable to contract.

Our pay was due us 3 weeks ago. The paymaster got the money to pay us and refunded it back to the treasurer again so we won't get paid for two & prehaps 4 months to come. I am unfortunately out of money & if you could send me six or eight doll's in your next letter it would help me greatly. Something may happen, I may be taken sick & need a little by me. I must bring this to a close. Please write often.

Your Aff'n't Son, Henry Matrau

Tell Frank I'll send him a novel as soon as I can get hold of one.
I am 4th Corps.[b]

a. *Saleratus* is sodium bicarbonate — baking soda.
b. This seems to be an error as the Black Hat Brigade was the Fourth *Brigade* in the First Division of I Corps at this time. See Nolan, 194.

Camp near Belle Plain Va March 3d/63
Dear Mother,

I received you[r] kind letter of the 20th ult. with the five dollars enclosed three day's ago & would have answered it sooner, but we had to go on picket duty the next day. I also received another letter from Frank yesterday with tea enclosed. I hav'nt tried the tea yet but I think some of having a staving [bracing] old cup of tea tonight. If there is anything that makes a soldier feel good it is to think there [are] those at home who care for him & who are always thinking of his welfare. We have just been mustered for 4 months pay & should get paid about the 15th or so. I think the 5 doll's will be amply sufficient to last me. My health has been good all the winter & if it continues so, I think I shall be able to weather out my remaining 17 months first rate. It begins to look some like spring & the blue birds are beginning to come out from their winter haunts. I got a letter from Aunt Sarah near a month ago & answered it, but it was probably miscarried & never reached its destination. I will write her a letter to day if I can. Tell brother Frank it has been so long scince I attempted to write a composition that I fear I should make poor work of it. I have a book though I will send him. It is rather the worse for wear but is nevertheless a bully good story. When you write, please tell me all about the farm & what is going on in the neighborhood. I must bring this to a close. Please write soon.

Your Aff'nte Son, H. Matrau

Belle Plain Va. March 17th/63

Dear Mother,

Your kind letter of the 9th came to hand day before yesterday. I am always glad to hear from home, especially to hear you are all well. I wrote you a letter immediately on receiving the one with the money, which it seems you had not received. I am as well as usual. The weather is growing warm fast, the roads are drying up and we'll probably be on the war path soon.

It is queer what stories will get afloat about army movements. The left grand Division has not to my knowledge had any intentions of going farther south, more than it has of going to the moon. I don't think it would be a very good plan to send a box now, mother, for t'would take it two weeks to come through & likely e're that time we will be on the move and I could'nt get it. We will probably get into a big fight one of these day's & maybe I'll get a commission and maybe a broken leg, the latter the more likely of the two. But you must keep up good spirits, mother, and pray for the best.

I have received several packages from Mrs Yund. Please tell her I thank her very much & will write to them. Ask Lucy if she thinks she would know me in my soger rig with my knapsack, haversack, canteen, and cartridge box on. I think she'd have to look twice. I had a staving old cup of tea of that you sent me last night. I hav'nt drank a better in a long time. I mailed the Irish Dragoon to Frank the other day. Tell Morgan I should really like to get a letter from him. I must bring this to a close. Please write soon.

Your Affectionate son, Henry Matrau.

Belle Plain Va Apr 3d/63

Dear Aunt[a]

I received your kind letter of the 22d ult yesterday & was very glad to hear from you, I tell you, & glad to hear that you were enjoying good health. I am as well as usual & as tough as salt junk & hard tack can make a man. We are still in our winter quarters but how much longer we will stay in them I cant tell.

I may as well tell you what kind of a place this Belle Plain is. It is no place at all but a sort of steamboat landing & military depot for the Commissary & quatermaster's stores for the Army.

The *town* is composed of 15 or 20 huge Commissary tents, 8 or 10 log huts, & a sort of quay or wharf. It is such a town as few in civil life have the opportunity of seeing for wherever we go this town goes with us. We have nothing to do nowadays but drill ocasionally, inspection three times a week, & guard & picket duty. We were reviewed yesterday by Gen. Hooker.[b] The order to march generally follows close after a review so we are looking for a forward movement every day.

It would take me a good while to give anything like an accurate account of my travels scince I left home. I came by rail to Washington from Madison Wis & scince then shanks horses[c] have propelled me over many a weary mile of Virginia soil. I have been in three battles, I have smelt powder, heard the music of the bullet, listened to the roar of canonade, dodged bombshells, have seen my comrades shot down by my side while I remained unhurt, in short I've seen the elephant[d] & now want to go home & fight a duel with *Rhoda*'s man & end this war in a glorious peace.

But I suppose I will have to fight a few more battles & do some more dodgeing before I can do that. It seems that the Misses Rubles are not married yet so I have something to live for at all events, for I was strongly tempted to shoot myself when I heard what Rhoda had done. Does the old Good Templar Lodge meet as it used to or has it broken up? Do you know where John Worden is & what he is doing? Is you[r] brother James in the army or not? Do they baptize as many in big Paw Paw lake as they used to? Does Mr Warren keep [the] boot & shoe shop at his old place yet? But I must bring this to a close. Please write soon & tell me all the news. Give my love to Uncle Henry & Georgie.

Your Affectionate Nephew, Henry Matrau.

a. The wife of Uncle Henry, Amanda's half brother

b. On April 2, the First Division paraded for Generals Hooker and Wadsworth, and a few days later President and Mrs. Lincoln arrived to review the troops. The Iron Brigade's fame was such that the president specifically spoke of them to General Hooker. See Nolan, 206–8.

c. *Shank's horses*, or more commonly *Shank's Mare*, to walk, from the German word *schenken*.

d. "To see the elephant" was a common nineteenth-century expression from the circus, where the animal was a prime attraction. Therefore, to see the elephant was to have seen everything. See Jay Monaghan, ed., *The Book of the American West* (New York: Bonanza Books, 1958), 523.

Chapter Four

Letters of May 1, 1863, to September 17, 1863

GENERAL HOOKER'S plan for a spring offensive consisted of a pincer movement. While Gibbons's division remained in front of Fredericksburg, three corps would move down the Rappahannock. As part of this diversion, Reynolds's I Corps, including the Sixth Wisconsin, would cross the river below Fredericksburg. Meanwhile, the rest of the army would circle north and west, cross the Rappahannock and Rapidan rivers, and attack Lee's forces from the rear.[1]

Having successfully completed these movements, Hooker's men encountered the Confederates in the wilderness area west of Fredericksburg, but Lee's spirited defense brought them to a standstill. Hooker called for reinforcements, including Reynolds's I Corps. As in the preceding year, the Iron Brigade served as the rear guard for the move back across the river, pickets again crossing in boats after the bridge was withdrawn. They marched north, recrossed the river, and arrived to take up defensive positions near Chancellorsville but were not called upon to fight.[2]

Lee and Stonewall Jackson outgeneralled and outfought Hooker in spite of inferior numbers. Jackson's march to Hooker's right flank caught Howard's XI Corps completely by surprise, although there were frequent reports of the movement (some from spotters in balloons tethered at the scene). Hooker discounted them, insisting that Jackson was retreating.[3]

General Hooker's lack of experience in directing large-scale maneuvers had become apparent even before he was wounded while standing on the balcony of Chancellor House. He retired briefly from the field, leaving General Couch in command of a withdrawal.[4] Lee subsequently drove Hooker and all the federal troops back across the Rappahannock and by May 7 the Iron Brigade was again camped east of Falmouth, near White Oak Church, where they had been on April 28.[5]

The Battle of Chancellorsville cost the South dearly, however. Stonewall Jackson was accidentally shot by his own men and died at Guinea's Station a few days later.

The big news was from the western front. Vicksburg, Mississippi, was located on a high bluff, commanding the great river and the traffic that traveled on it. Confederate General Pemberton had been driven into the strongly fortified city by Union General Grant, who circled behind and blocked off any chance of reinforcement by land. The siege of Vicksburg began in mid-May, 1863. With Union ships under Admiral Porter controlling the river, the citizens found themselves attacked by shelling from all sides. After six weeks, the city was reduced to rubble and the starving populace was living in caves and basements. On July 4, the last day of the Battle of Gettysburg, Pemberton finally surrendered.[6]

May and June marked the end of two-year enlistment terms for many regiments. I Corps lost almost five thousand men; Wadsworth's division had been reduced from nineteen to eleven regiments. They were consolidated into two brigades instead of the previous four, and the Iron Brigade became number one. It therefore became the First Brigade of the First Division of the First Corps and assumed custodianship of the division flag.[7]

Finally, in June the Confederate troops again moved north toward Maryland and Pennsylvania. After initial confusion as to Lee's intentions, the federal army also broke camp and marched past Washington, changing commanders as they went. General George G. Meade replaced Hooker following a confrontation between Hooker and authorities in Washington.[8] The extremely hot weather and the forced pace of the march resulted in many casualties among the troops. General Wadsworth ordered the ambulances cleared of officers' belongings so they could be loaded with the knapsacks and muskets of the men.[9]

On June 30, I Corps reached the Pennsylvania line at Emmitsburg, north of Frederick. They were the vanguard of the Union Army. Ahead lay the main body of Confederates centered at Chambersburg, about twenty-five miles to the northwest. Between was the little town of Gettysburg.

The location of the battle was sheer chance. Meade and Lee both intended to take strong defensive positions and await attack, but a unit of Southern soldiers moving toward Gettysburg in search of shoes and boots met Buford's Northern cavalry brigade west of town.[10] Immediately behind the cavalry was General Reynolds's I Corps with Cutler's brigade leading the march and the Iron Brigade following. Reynolds sent a message to Meade and then led an attack. He was killed by a sharpshooter's bullet and the momentum of the fighting started to turn. The situation was reversed, however, when Lieutenant Colonel Rufus Dawes brought up the last reserves of the Iron Brigade, including the Sixth Wisconsin. (Dawes had assumed command of the regiment when Colonel Bragg was injured by a horse the previous month.[11]) The renewed attack swept over the Confederates, trapped them in a railroad cut, and resulted in the surrender of 230 men, including seven officers.[12]

As the day progressed, more Southern troops arrived and the Federals were forced to withdraw slowly, moving up the exposed slopes of Seminary Ridge to a rail-fence barricade. The Iron Brigade maintained this new position while most of the corps retreated through town to Cemetery Ridge and Culp's Hill. They then retired in orderly fashion, although suffering heavy casualties. At last, the survivors regrouped and joined the entrenching efforts already under way. The Confederates did not attack and that night the rest of Meade's army reached the scene. During the remaining days of the battle the brigade played a reduced part.[13]

Lee attacked again on July 2, causing heavy Union losses, but Meade held fast. On July 3, the Battle of Gettysburg reached its climax with Pickett's charge on the Union center. It was a disaster and led to Lee's withdrawal the following day. In spite of urgent messages from Lincoln, Meade did not counterattack and the beaten Southern army crossed the Potomac to safety a few days later. Meade followed shortly thereafter.[14]

The Iron Brigade suffered 65 percent casualties during the battle. (Some regiments were practically destroyed — the Twenty-fourth Michigan had casualties of 80 percent.) According to the official records, the Sixth Wisconsin lost 168 men. General Meredith, the brigade commander, was severely wounded, and of fourteen field officers, only five remained on duty.[15] Gettysburg was really the end of the old western Iron Brigade, since those lost were replaced by men from various states.[16] The name remained, but its unique character was lost.

Nonetheless, the Iron Brigade's fame had spread widely through newspaper reports of the war. After Gettysburg, a piece of music entitled "The Iron Brigade Quickstep" even made an appearance.[17]

The losses at Gettysburg necessitated new command arrangements. Reynolds was replaced by General John Newton as corps commander. First Division commander Wadsworth went on extended sick leave until the following spring, and his position was shared by Cutler and others, since Meredith was also out. Meredith returned in October but had to withdraw permanently from field command two weeks later. Meanwhile, Cutler also shared the brigade command with Colonel Robinson. The Sixth Wisconsin's Colonel Bragg was still unable to resume field command, so Rufus Dawes continued in his temporary position.[18]

* * *

In the trenches on the Richmond
side of the Rappahannock

May 1st 1863.

Dear Parents,

I take the opportunity of an interval in the shelling operations of rebels to write you a few lines to let you know I am still alive & well. We broke up camp at Belle plain Monday the 28th at noon & camped for the night near the river, 4 miles below Fredericksburg. We went to bed & were routed out about 10 oclock & marched down to the river with the pontoons. We lay on the bank till daylight, when the 22d N.Y. commenced putting the pontoons in water. They had got one boat in the water when the Rebs opened on them from their rifle pits on the opposite side of the river. The 22d just got up & run & left boats, wagons, & drivers to shift for themselves. The boat that was in the water drifted to the other side. We marched down to a stone wall & let into them, & for a while it was give & take, till the 1st brigade came down & we moved back a little way where we lay down, & as we had had no sleep at all the previous night, most of us went to sleep & our batteries commenced shelling. In about an hour we were woke up & told to fall in, with nothing but our guns & cartridge boxes on. Our Col. [Edward S. Bragg] then told us that we were to march down to the river bank, then make a rush for the boats & paddle across & drive the rebs from their pits & breastworks. It was a perilous job & our regiment was the first to cross. Well we could not stop to think of the danger but started on a keen run for the boats & piled into them & shoved off under the hottest musketry fire I have ever yet witnessed or ever wish to again. We reached the opposite shore & charged with a yell for their breastworks. We drove them out of these & up the bank at the point of the bayonet before any troops but our own regt were across.

We captured 207 pris. besides small arms & equipments.[a] The rebs fell back to their fortifications on the heigts. Our division only crossed. The rest of our Corps lay on the other side yet. To day is fryday & we have got a big line of earthworks thrown up fronting the rebs. They are as thick as bees in front of us in their works but hav'nt given us any trouble beyond a little artillery practice. I expect they will renew this pleasant pastime soon. The largest portion of our army has gone in another direction, where, I dont know, but we expect to hold our position at all hazards. I must close, excuse any more for the present. Give my love to the family & all enquiring friends & tell the copperheads[b] that the army of the Potomac is'nt demoralized yet.

Your Affcnt. son, Henry Matrau.

a. Henry's claim of 207 prisoners is at odds with the official record of 90. In fact, his statement that the Sixth Wisconsin was the first regiment across the river is in dispute because the Twenty-fourth Michigan also claimed the honor. Actually, as the historian for the latter stated, "It was a neck and neck race between two friendly regiments of the Iron Brigade . . . and there were bullets and glory enough for both." Once entrenched on the heights, the men settled in to endure an artillery bombardment and await further orders. See Nolan, 213–14, 314.

b. *Copperhead* was a derogatory slang term for Northerners who advocated making peace with the South and restoring the Union, even if it meant the continuation of slavery.

Camp on the east bank of the Rappahannock

May 9th/63

Dear Mother,

When I wrote you last we were on the other side of the river & quite proud of our little turn with the butternuts[a] but circumstances have somewhat altered our position scince then. On the 2d inst we left our trenches & retreated back across the river. The rebels brought one gun to bear on us & smashed a pontoon as we were crossing the river but fortunately we lost not a man in our movement. The order to evacuate our position was caused by orders from Gen. Hooker to reinforce the center which Gen. Lee was trying to break. We in our corps accordingly marched up the river to Kelly's ford where we crossed on the morning of the 3d and marched about 4 miles into the interior of the country where we lay as a sort of reserve behind the first line of battle till the morning of the 6th at 2 oclock when we were woke up, ordered to pack up & prepare to march.

It had commenced raining the night previous & the whole country was flooded. As soon as our faces were turned to the river, we knew it was the old story, retreating from a superior foe. The roads were awful muddy, one of my shoes stuck in the mud. I gave my foot a jerk & it came to the surface minus the shoe. I durst'nt fall out for fear of being picked up by Stuart's cavalry so I picked up my shoe & trudged on through the mud & rain about a mile where we halted & I put the refractory shoe on. We crossed the river a little after daylight & marched to Harwood Church where we camped for the night. The next morning we resumed our march and traveled down the river to nearly opposite the place where we crossed [on] the 29th, where we are now encamped. How soon we will move again no one can tell. I am as well as usual & have stood the tramp firstrate for a youth. I think Gen. Hooker has done better than any other General in the army could have done.

I must bring this to a close.

I saw Merritt Enos[b] while we were laying in line of battle. He was as tough and hearty as usual & looked as rugged as a bear.

Please write often.

Yours truly, Henry Matrau

a. *Butternuts* refers to the Confederate soldiers, whose uniforms were dyed with an extract from the butternut, or white oak tree.

b. The Enos family were pioneer settlers in Bainbridge. James H. Enos held the positions of town clerk and justice of the peace.

Camp near White Oak Church June 2d/63

Dear Mother,

I rec'd your kind letter of the 23d ult yesterday & was glad to hear from home. We were on picket when I rec'd your letter. We were on pick[et] right on the bank of the Rappahanock river & the reb pickets were on the opposite side within talking distance & although the orders are strictly against our pickets conversing with theirs, still a strange yet friendly dialogue is often carried on, in the absence of officers, & papers sometimes exchanged. This morning before we were relieved a rebel sergeant swam over with a yesterday's Richmond paper & exchanged it for one of our papers, talked a while, & swam back again.

The first thing he asked was what the news we had from Vicksburg was. We told him that from the last accounts it appeared to be in a pretty tight fix.

I am as well as usual and hope good health will not desert me while I stay in the army. We are still laying in the same camp that we were in when I wrote you last. When the Army of the Potomac will again be put in motion & what end it is to accomplish is hard to say. Our force is greatly diminished by the expiration of the time of the 2 yrs and 9 months men who have gone home & who are still going and we see none to take their place. What can be done to fill up the vacancy?

I rec'd that letter you spoke about but not till after I had written & sent that one you received. You spoke in it about a certain Geo. Jay. He deserted while we were laying near Alexandria over a year ago. Yes, he basely deserted his comrades who are now, alas, many mouldering under the sod & the rest willing to take their chance of life or death in our country's service. I like to have Morgan write for it seems as if I could hear him crack the ox whip & sing out "whoahaw, Buck!" when I read his letters. I must close, tis near tatoo beat. Give my love to the family and all enquiring friends and please write soon and tell me all the news and current items.

Your aff'nt son, H. C. Matrau.

Camp near Guilford Sta Va – June 20th/63

Dear Mother,

I take this short interval of rest from hard marching to let you know I am still alive and well & not altogether the worse for wear.

Scince I wrote you last the Grand Army has made an important move to avert, I suppose, the threatened invasion of Pennsylvania and Maryland. We broke camp on the Rappahannock early on the morning of the 13th inst & marched up the river to near Harwood Church a distance of about 12 miles where we stopped for dinner. This was the day appointed for the execution of private John P. Woods of the 19th Ind Reg for desertion to the enemy. He was sentenced to be shot to death by musketry and was brought along in an ambulance, heavily ironed & under a heavy guard. After we had got our dinner we fell into line and marched out on an open field and our division was formed in a sort of hollow triangle around a slight hollow. Two ambulances then drove into the square, one with the prisoner and the other with the coffin, followed by the guard & a squad of men with picks and spades to dig the grave. He got out of the ambulance and about half an hour was spent by the chaplain talking & praying with him. The coffin was placed on the ground, the prisoner took his seat on it and a white handkerchief [was] tied around his eyes. Twelve men then formed a line in front of him, the command was given to fire, a rattling volley followed & the guilty one was no more. Life did not appear to be totally extinct & two men put two bullets through his heart to finish the tragedy.

We left the men digging his grave and resumed the march as if nothing had happened.

The 19th Ind belongs to our brigade. We camped for the

night at a mill 10 miles from the church. From there we went to Beale Sta., then to Manassas junction, then to Centerville, then to Herndon Sta, then to Guilford Sta on the Alexandria & Leesburg R.R., where we are now sojourning. We have been out 8 days, marching most of the time, one night all night without any sleep. I have stood it first rate so far, notwithstanding the extreme heat. Several men have been sun struck in our division. What the results of this movement will [be] none of us have the least idea. I must bring this to a close. Please write soon & tell all the news. Give my love to the family & all enquiring friends.

Your Affnte son, H. C. Matrau.

Warrenton Junction July 29th/63

Dear Parents,

It has been a long time scince I have written to you but I tell you we have had a rough old time for the last month & a half. We have been on the tramp all of the time, only stopping long enough at a place to eat & sleep & fight a battle. Have had no chance to wash our clothes or anything else. I would have written before but I could'nt get paper & envelopes. We had a hard fight at Gettysburg and a merciful Providence has again taken me through the ordeal of battle unscathed. Our brigade were the first engaged on the 1st of July. We were ordered to "trail arms, doublequick march, and load as you run." A brigade of rebels lay in a railroad cut. Our reg't charged on them under a galling fire of musketry, drove them, & captured the 2nd Miss. regt, their Major, & colors.

We captured 160 more men than we went into the fight with. In this first day's fight we lost 30 killed & 138 wounded. Our company had 4 killed & 8 wounded out of 27 we went into the fight with. The rest of the fight, how we were outflanked on both sides & fell back through the town you already know as well as I can tell you. The battle field of Gettysburg was one vast slaughter pen. Dead & wounded lay in all directions. A man that went through the carnage unhurt may call himself a lucky man. My health is still good, I would like a little rest though. Tell father I would as soon throw my old musket down & take a turn at farming as not.

I must close. Please write soon & tell me all the news. Give my love to the children & all enquiring friends.

Your Aff'nte Son, Henry C. Matrau

Rappahannock Sta Va Aug 12th/63

Dear Aunt Sarah,

It has been a good while scince I have written to you but we have had a long & arduous campaign and I have not even written home as often as I ought to have done, so that must in part excuse me from dilatoriness.

We have chased old Lee over many a weary mile of hill & dale, woodland & desert, (mostly desert in Virginia,) but we came on him all of a sudden one fine morning among the wheat fields of Penn. and had a game of "roll the trenches" on about as magnificent a scale as has ever been played on this continent. We were the first troops engaged on the 1st of July & that day we lost two thirds of our number killed & wounded. When we came up to the scene of action we were ordered "forward in line, double quick march, load as you run." It was sharp work, I tell you, & old Sol was pouring down his hottest rays. The 147th N.Y. Reg't were driven back by the rebs & we were detached from the old Iron Brigade to take the ground they had lost. A brigade of rebs lay in a railroad cut with just their heads visible, pouring a perfect storm of bullets into us & our men were falling in every direction. We charged on them, drove them, & captured the entire 2nd Miss. Reg't. It was dearly bought but nobly done. You know the rest, how we were outflanked & outnumbered 5 to one & had to fall back & take a new position. Our corps lost fearfuly. I am in good health with the exception of a few boils & have never been touched by a bullet yet. I must close. Please write soon & tell me all the news.

Your Affnte Nephew, H. C. Matrau.

Rappahannock Sta Va Aug 16/63

Dear Mother,

The Capt of my company [Philip W. Plummer] received a letter from you a few days ago asking my whereabouts & whether I [was] alive or among the many missing. I wrote a letter about two weeks previous which you probbably have rec'd ere this. The reason I did'nt write sooner was our being on the move continually, & writing materials were impossible to be had for love or money. We are now encamped near Rappahannock Sta but are under orders to be ready to march at a moments notice.

How long we will stay here we cant tell. We may leave in an hour & we may stay 3 months. I am as well as usual with the exeption of a few boils.

We had an awful hot time at Gettysburg but it does seem as if I was the luckiest fellow in existence. There were men falling in every direction around me & the best hearted fellow in our company was killed right close to me, so near that he nearly fell on to me. I must come to a close. Please write soon.

Your Affnte son, H. C. Matrau

Rappahannock Sta Va Aug 22nd/63

Dear Mother,

I received your kind letter on the 13th & was glad to hear that the folks at home were still enjoying a tolerable portion of good health. But death, it seems, makes inroads as well in the peaceful hamlet as in the relentless strife of the bloody battle field.

I sometimes think I shall hardly know my native place, there have been so many changes scince I left it.

So many old familiar faces gone & new ones probably in their place, old buildings torn down & new ones built up. Woodland I used to make reverberate with the music of "our old shotgun" transformed into broad fields of waving grain will make the old place so changed I'm afraid I should hardly know it.

I am still enjoying good health, which is a great blessing to a soldier. We were on picket yesterday about a mile and a half the other side of the river. There was a rebel camp in plain sight of our post. What our future movements will be no one can tell. There [are] a thousand & one different rumors going about camp. Some say the army will fall back to Washington but no one knows. I must bring this to a close. Please write soon & tell me all the news & what the people around there think of the conscript act.[a] Give my love to the children & all enquiring friends.

Your Aff'nte son, Henry Matrau.

a. As the war progressed, it became apparent that volunteers could not fill the places left vacant by casualties and desertion. Therefore, on March 3, 1863, Congress passed the first national conscription act, which provided that all men between eighteen and forty-five had to register for military service (Morison, 666). A furor arose over this sweeping usurpation of states' rights by the federal government. (Ironically, Southern governors were equally incensed with Jefferson Davis over a similar law.) See Catton, *Glory Road*, 136–38.

The act provided for only two methods of exemption: a fee in lieu of service for a particular draft, or permanent exemption by procuring a substitute who would sign up for three years. Obviously, this system was unfair to the poor and in July, when the first names were drawn in working-class areas of New York, rioting broke out. Troops had to be detached from the front line to restore order and guard property in several cities. In fact, it has been suggested that this was one reason Meade did not resume the offensive at Gettysburg. See Morison, 666–67.

Recruits were credited to the districts in which they enlisted, so state agents scoured occupied areas of the South, city slums, and even poorhouses in Europe. Federal officials were bribed to accept criminals and the mentally and physically handicapped. Needless to say, the arrival of this sort of replacement caused morale problems among the members of veteran volunteer regiments. See Bruce Catton, *A Stillness at Appomattox*, vol. 3 of *The Army of the Potomac* (Garden City: Doubleday, 1953), 24–26; Morison, 667.

Camp near Culpepper Va Sept 17th/63

Dear Parents,

I have written two letters home & received none in return, & I begin to think "the old folks at home" have nearly or quite forgotten their truant son down in the old Dominion. I have been looking every day as the mail came in for a letter from home & you dont know what a long physiog[nomy] it puts on a soger to hear all the names called & his own left out in the cold. Scince I wrote you last, our Corps has moved across the Rappahanack to within about 3 miles of Culpepper Court house. We got here about 2 p.m. yesterday. We started [at] 5 A.M. yesterday & travelled quite brisk.

Gen. Lee is said to be falling back towards Richmond.

Our pickets are on this side of [the] Rapidan river, posted along the bank. I am in as good health & as tough as usual. We are all looking for a fight soon but we cant tell, we may go into winter quarters without fighting. One thing is certain, if Gen. Lee attacks us, he will have as tough a piece of business to perform as he ever undertook in his life.

I have been promoted to Sergeant scince I wrote you last.[a] When you write again I wish you would give me Uncle Philo's address & Cousin Angeline's also, I have forgotten both. When you write again have Morgan & Frank write to [me] & [ask] Morgan to tell me about his live stock & Frank about any thing else he has a mind to. We are going to have a brigade flag presentation this afternoon. The flag was made in N.Y. city & is presented by the states of Wis, Mich, & Indiana, the brigade being composed of regiments from those states.[b] We are now known as the Iron Brigade, I believe now throughout the army. I must bring this to a close. Please write soon.

Your Affnte son, Henry C. Matrau.

a. Henry was promoted to sergeant on September 13, 1863. (Pension and Military Records of Henry C. Matrau, NARS.)
b. The flag was commissioned by the citizens of Wisconsin, Michigan, and Indiana residing in Washington, D.C., and presented to the brigade on the anniversary of Antietam (see Nolan, 265).

1. Private Henry C. Matrau, Company G, Sixth
Wisconsin Volunteer Infantry, taken July 5, 1862, at
Fredericksburg, Virginia. Collection of the editor.

2. Captain Henry C. Matrau,
photograph taken in 1865 at Petersburg,
Virginia. Collection of the editor.

3. Henry C. Matrau, his wife Jerusha, and their children
(from left) Agnes, Harry, Ruth, Mary, and Grace, in Norfolk,
Nebraska in the 1890s. Collection of the editor.

4. Henry C. Matrau in the Nebraska state legislature, 1911.
Collection of the editor.

Chapter Five

Letters of October 22, 1863, to June 26, 1864

As the Armies of the Potomac and Northern Virginia moved south during the fall of 1863 they were in frequent contact with each other. Skirmishes occurred but no major battles developed and casualties were light.[1]

In October, Lee attacked Meade, whose forces had been reduced as units were detached for the western campaign. He forced a retreat but was unable to prevent Meade's arrival at a fortified position behind Bull Run.[2] General Meade retaliated with a surprise offensive in November, but his movements were detected by Southern cavalry. Consequently, Meade found Lee in a strongly fortified position on the bank of Mine Run in the wilderness. He withdrew and the two armies entered winter camps at a stalemate.[3]

Meanwhile, in the west Grant's forces had routed the enemy at Chattanooga. In March, Lincoln promoted Grant to lieutenant general and brought him to Washington as general-in-chief. Meade continued in his position as commander of the Army of the Potomac, but Grant established his headquarters with Meade and took direct control of planning for the spring campaign.

His first order of business was to reorganize the army and combine units that had been reduced by heavy casualties.

Meade's force was consolidated into three corps. The old I Corps, which had never recovered from Gettysburg, was divided in two — the Second and Fourth divisions, each containing four brigades — and absorbed by Major General Gouvernour K. Warren's V Corps. In recognition of their previous status, they were allowed to retain their old corps badges. James Wadsworth returned to duty as commander of the Fourth Division and Lysander Cutler assumed command of the First Brigade, including the five regiments of the old Iron Brigade.[4]

On May 4, Grant set in motion his plan to attack the Southern forces on several fronts. The two largest federal forces were Sherman's, moving across Georgia and then north, and Meade's, moving south from winter camp at Culpeper. Grant personally accompanied Meade's troops and was in command of the operation.

The first clash between Lee and Grant took place May 5 through 7 around Wilderness Tavern, to the west of the old Chancellorsville battlefield. The terrain was heavily wooded and very uneven with alternately hilly and swampy areas, an ideal situation for Lee's smaller defending army. A special horror was fire and smoke as the dry brush burst into flames. Several times, fighting stopped while soldiers tried to save the wounded. The battle ended in a draw, although federal forces had heavier casualties than the Southerners. The Iron Brigade was in the center of the heaviest fighting and suffered severely. Among the casualties was divisional commander Wadsworth, who was killed on the second day. Brigadier General Cutler replaced him, while Colonel Robinson of the Seventh Indiana took over the brigade temporarily. In June, Edward Bragg was promoted to brigadier general and assumed permanent command.[5]

Lee expected Grant to withdraw as the previous Northern commanders had done in similar situations. Instead, he moved his men to the east and continued to march toward the Confederate capitol of Richmond. Lee withdrew to Spotsylvania and dug in to meet them.

This was the beginning of a campaign that differed from those of earlier years. The two armies were in almost continual contact and never separated to rest and recover. Grant stated that he was going to hammer at the enemy and his resources until attrition gave him the victory that individual battles could not.[6]

The Battle of Spotsylvania started on May 8 and developed into trench warfare.[7] Confederate General Ewell occupied a point called the Mule Shoe (because of its shape), but on May 12, Union forces attacked with such ferocity that it became known as "the Bloody Angle." As Henry reports, the Sixth Wisconsin charged the west flank of this salient and was again in heavy fighting. For twenty hours, the two armies shot at each other; they were so close the battle flags almost touched across the parapet separating them. Finally, after midnight, Ewell withdrew under cover of darkness and rain.[8]

More attacks and skirmishes followed until the armies disengaged on May 20. It was an indecisive ending but once again Grant moved left and continued his push to the south, hoping to entice Lee into attacking.[9] Lee, however, interpreted Grant's plans correctly and moved by a direct route to the North Anna River where he entrenched. Portions of the federal army, including Cutler's division, managed to cross the river but found Lee's position too strong to assault successfully.[10] Grant withdrew the night of May 26–27 and, crossing the Pamunkey, moved to Totopotomay Creek only to find Lee blocking him once more. On May 30, the Sixth Wisconsin was involved in action at Bethesda Church, successfully repelling a Confederate attack. The next night, both Grant and Lee moved south to Cold Harbor, a crossroads village on the road to Richmond.[11]

Lee took a strong stand in heavily fortified breastworks, but Grant decided to attack boldly. He was concerned about his army's mental and physical exhaustion after a month of marching and fighting but was sure that the Confederates were even more demoralized. He was wrong. The battle on June 3 was a disaster for the North, reminiscent of Fredericksburg, and Grant the hero became Grant "the butcher." No one regretted it more than he. It is said he spent the following night weeping in his tent. Luckily for the Sixth Wisconsin, it was stationed at the far right of the Union line and escaped the heaviest concentration of fire. The lines faced each other until June 7, when Grant initiated a truce to allow both sides to rescue the wounded who had managed to survive.[12]

Five days later, Grant turned his back on Lee, crossed the James River and marched to take Petersburg, thus cutting off the supplies reaching Lee through that important rail center. Secrecy was of the utmost importance, and by making feints toward Richmond, Grant managed to move his large army without being detected. When the first Union detachments reached Petersburg, the city was defended by a very small force under General Beauregard. The Union generals on the scene hesitated while Grant was still busy directing the river crossing. The opportunity was lost as reinforcements started to reach Beauregard. After several assaults with heavy losses on June 15 through 18, the Union Army built fortifications around the city, facing the Confederates in their trenches. The siege of Petersburg began.[13]

* * *

Thoroughfare Gap Oct 22nd/63

Dear Parents,

I received your kind letter of the 2nd a few day's ago, but we have been marching all of the time & I have had no chance to answer it. I am as tough as ever, & as saucy, too, for backing 8 day's ration's dont improve a man's temper a bit. I may as well tell you about the moves we have had for the last two weeks. We commenced the retreat from the [near Culpeper, Virginia] somewhere about the 12th, & there for the first time, we stood where we could see other troops fighting & were not called upon to participate. I suppose the rebs were trying to flank us but we got to Centerville ahead of them & for once frustrated their designs if such they were. We lay at Centerville for a while & the baffled rebs were retreating back towards the Rappahanock when we cut stick[a] & followed them. We are now camped at thoroughfare Gap in the Bull Run Mountains about 18 miles from Warrenton.

We hav'nt been in an engagement through the whole affair but have had some pretty severe marching.

I should like to be at home to help eat some of the nice peaches & apples but will have to content myself with persimmons for a while yet.

So another bachelor uncle of mine has got married.[b] Wa'll, I suppose I will have more aunts & cousin's to get aquainted with when I get home than I can shake a stick at. I saw James Boughton of St Jo a day or two ago. He is Lieut. in the 7th Mich Cav. I get 17 dollars a month now. I must bring this to a close. Please write soon.

Your Affn'te son, Henry Matrau.

a. To "cut stick" is to leave hurriedly or secretly.
b. One of Amanda's brothers.

Camp near Kelley's Ford Va Dec 7th/63

Dear Mother,

I received your kind letter of Nov 30th & was glad to hear that the folks at home were doing well. Scince I wrote you last we have had another short campaign but a hard one in marching & inclement weather.

We crossed the Rappahanock on 27 ult & marched across the country to Germanna ford on the Rapidan, where we camped that night. The next morning we crossed the river on pontoons before daylight & marched on by-roads through a dense forrest of scrubby pines, denominated the Wilderness, till we got on the Fredericksburg & Orange Court House plank road, which we took & struck off in the direction of the Court House. We were marching in the rear of the 5th Corps wagon train about 10 AM when they were attacked by about 100 Reb Cavalry. Our Regt deployed as skirmishers through the wood on each side of the road & moved forward to the train. There the Rebs were drinking whiskey, rummaging wagons, cutting mules loose, whipping the teamsters, & raising the devil generally. But they got more spirits than counted on, for the old 6th let a volley into them that emptied a dozen or twenty saddles & set them running for dear life. They, however, had set fire to a dozen wagons loaded with shells that commenced a series of explosions that is not very often witnessed on a Fourth of July celebration. We continued our march to Robertsons Tavern where we halted for the night. There we formed a line of battle & advanced through the woods, the Rebs falling back all the time to the other side of mile run [Mine Run] on a range of Heights well fortified. To have charged those Heigts with the number of men we had would have been sheer murder & Gen. Meade knew it. So we fell back to our old position. We are now on the west side of the Rappahanock & are building winter quaters.

Whether we will stay here to enjoy them or not we cant tell. When you write, if you can get a copy of the St Jo paper without too much trouble, I would like to have you send me one. I must close, please write soon.

Your Affetn son, H. C. Matrau

[February 1864]ᵃ

Dear Father,

I arrived safe in Millwaukee yesterday. The Reg't isn't all here yet, they are coming in, though, as fast as they can. We are going into camp here about 3 miles out of town. We will probably leave in a few day's for [the] seat of war. I will write again as soon as we are settled. If you can send me 5 dolls I would like it.

Direct to Millwaukee Wis. I dont know as there will be any local bounty here at all. Please write as soon as you [can] & put on the envelope To follow Reg't, Give love to children,

Your son, H. C. Matrau

a. Since the Sixth Wisconsin left Milwaukee on February 22, 1864, the letter was probably written during the preceding week or two.

Washington Feb 26th 1864

Dear Mother,

I arrived in Washington last night, 12 oclock, safe & sound & a little bit tired of riding on the car's. We left Milwaukee the morning of the Anniversary of the birthday of Washington. I received Franks letter telling me of Morgans arrival home the day before we left, but we were in such a hurry & bustle preparing to leave, making out reports, etc., that I had'nt time to hear myself think, much less to write. Tell Morgan I was very sorry I could'nt see him but I hope & pray he may allways be as lucky as his brother Hank has been.[a]

I must tell you now of another streak of luck I've had. The cars ran off the track in Penn. near Perry'sville while we were going at the rate of 35 miles an hour. I was in the front car, which was thrown off the track & smashed all to pieces, & the only man hurt was a brakesman who had his leg all smashed to pieces. The car's sent the ties & railroad iron in every direction for about 20 rods. We were riding on the bank of the Juniata river & 1 foot more would have sent us 70 feet down the bank into the river. But for my usual good luck & a merciful Providence I would have been in eternity ere now.

Wisconsin is using the Veteran's very meanly. They have been to work and got us credited to whatever town they had a mind to, & we can whistle for our bounty. They may conclude to pay 50 dolls in Beloit some time but I doubt it.[b] We will probably stay here 2 or 3 day's to draw guns, &c, for our recruits. Hundreds of men are coming into Washington every day for Our Army of the Potomac. There are 4000 here now waiting for transportation to the front. When you write I wish you would send me about 20 postage stamp's. I must close. Please write soon. Tell Frank I'll write to him as soon as a can. My love to all the family & all enq friends.

Your Affnte Son, H. C. Matrau

(direct as usual)

a. Morgan Matrau enlisted in Company B of the 12th Michigan Infantry at Kalamazoo, December 29, 1863.

b. By now, the enlistment period of the three-year men was drawing to a close and the federal high command wished to avoid repetition of their experience in the spring, when so many two-year regiments left the army. To persuade the soldiers to reenlist, Congress passed the Veteran Volunteer Act (see Boatner, 870). It authorized a bounty of four hundred dollars (to be paid in installments), the special title "veteran volunteer," and a red and blue service chevron for each man who signed up for three more years or the duration of the war. In addition, states offered local bounties so that the average soldier could expect to get around seven hundred dollars. The most valuable prize, however, was an immediate thirty-day furlough. If three-fourths of the regiment reenlisted, the men could take these furloughs at the same time and upon their return the regiment would retain its identity (see Catton, *A Stillness at Appomattox*, 34).

A great deal of pressure was applied to men of some regiments, whereas other officers were more restrained in presenting the option to the troops. The men of the Sixth Wisconsin took part in a sober and careful discussion on December 20, and by January 2 the quota had been met.

Those who reenlisted returned to a welcoming ceremony in Milwaukee and then dispersed to their homes (see Nolan, 267–71). The undated letter from Henry was obviously written in mid-February 1864 when he returned to the regiment after his furlough.

As to the bounty, military records show that Henry received one hundred dollars when he mustered out in December, 1863, and then was granted four hundred dollars for reenlisting. This was to be paid in installments of fifty dollars and he received the first three by the middle of 1864. One followed, but the last four were still due when he was mustered out of the service in 1865 (see Pension and Military Records of Henry C. Matrau, NARS).

Camp near Culpepper Va March 18th/64

Dear Father and Mother,

I received a letter from Mrs Yund yesterday and was very sorry to hear that you were having such a hard time with sickness in the family. It seems that Bainbridge has rather more than its share of sickness. I am afraid that you will wear yourselves out entirely taking care of the children but I trust that all of their lives may be spared.

I am sorry that Morgan went away looking so bad but I think that a change of climate will do him good. If Morgan's regiment stay's in Arkansas they won't see much fighting, for the big battles of this war will be fought in Tennesee and Virginia. When you write, I wish you would give me Morgan's address, also Uncle Philo's. When I was in Milwaukee I wrote for some money, for then I did not know how long we would stay there, but now I dont need the money at all and if you have not already sent it you need not. We are camped at present about $2\frac{1}{2}$ miles from Culpepper. Everything is quiet in the army now but we cant tell how long this quiet will last. The old saying is "there is always a calm before the storm."

U. S. Grant has been promoted to Lieut. General and is to take command of the whole United States army.

The talk is that he is going to take command of the Army of the Potomac in person for the first Campaign. This is merely rumour, however, and we cant vouch for its truth.

The Rebels are getting a big army in the field but they are bound to get whipped in the end, for right must eventually conquer.

The weather is rather cool at present & a good fire dont come amiss, I tell you. We are kept busy now drilling recruits. They generally learn pretty easy but there are some rather green subjects among them & we have some great times laughing at them. The boy's tell them big bear and bull stories, which they listen to with eyes & ear's open, and believe as implicitly as if they read them out of the Bible. Those stamps you sent me came through all right. I must bring this to a close. Please write as soon as you can find time, [even] if it is only a few words. My love to the children.

From your Aff'nte Son, Henry C. Matrau

Camp near Culpepper Va March 26th/64

Dear Father and Mother,

I take this opportunity to write you a few lines to let you know I am all right at present and hope that these few lines will find you all well at home. There is nothing going on here now and the roads are a mixture of clay & water, forming a condiment generally known as mud. I sent to you this morning $40 by Adams express Co and directed it as usual to Care of B C Hoyt Esq of St Joseph. We were paid yesterday. We have never received any local bounty whatever and dont expect any. But I can get along without it. I intend to send every cent I can spare home.

I know I have been very foolish for the last 3 yrs spending my $ when there was no need for it.

Lieut Gen Grant is in the City of Culpepper now. No more passes or furlough's will be granted, & things begin to look some like a move. What will be the next act in this grand drama of war no one can tell, but may God grant success to our Grant. When you write, tell me if the money came through safe. Give my love to the children.

Your Affectionate Son, Henry C. Matrau

Camp on the field near Spottsylvania C H

May 15th/64

Dear Mother,

I will write you a few lines just to let you know that we have had some pretty hard fighting lately but I am all right yet. We left Culpepper the 4th & marched all day, crossed the Rapidan river at Germania ford. The 5th we fought nearly all day & on the whole got rather the worst of it.

We have been fighting for 10 day's now & I think on the whole the Rebs have got rather the worst of it. We have lost 160 men in our Regt killed and wounded. We have got six men in my company. I am well, but I almost wonder how I have stood it as well as I have. We dont have much chance to write. We have captured about 7,000 prisoners scince the campaign comenced & 21 pieces of artillery. I must close & go to building breastworks. our old Capt was promoted to Major & was killed. I suppose you recollect his name was H. P. Plummer [P. W. Plummer]. Our 1st and 2nd Lieut's[a] were both wounded. Excuse haste & please write soon.

Your Affnte Son, Henry C. Matrau.

a. James L. Converse was the first lieutenant of Company G, having become an officer in 1861 after starting service as an enlisted man. He survived his wound at Spotsylvania but was subsequently killed (see Dawes, 26, 170, 253, 261, 296). The second lieutenant was John Timmons. When Lieutenant Converse died, Timmons refused promotion because he planned to muster out at the end of his enlistment. (For more information, see Dawes, 170, 253, 256, 297, 301, 303, 305, 307, 309, 310.)

Camp in the trenches near Spottsylvania

May 30th/64[a]

Dear Cousin Rusha[b]

I received your kind letter of the 10th inst this morning and was very glad to hear from you. Scince I wrote you last we have had some hard marching and still harder fighting but a kind Providence has preserved me thus far unscathed while many of my comrade's are laying cold and ghastly corpses unburied & unmarked.

I have'nt time nor space to give you a detailed acct of the battles but will make a few extracts from my diary just to show you what we have done. Left Culpepper the 4th, crossed the Rapidan river at Germania Ford at noon, marched to the turnpike going to Fredericksburg & camped for the night.

5th, broke camp at daylight, marched 2 miles, formed line of battle, & attacked the enemy who were in a thick pine woods. The country in which we are in is known as the Wilderness. Fought all day & when night closed in had only gained $\frac{3}{4}$ths of a mile.

6th, advanced through the woods & attacked the enemy who were in rifle pits, got a severe raking from a masked battery, were repulsed & fell back & lost $\frac{3}{4}$ of mile gained yesterday.

7th, did nothing but clean our guns & wash the powder out

of our faces In the evening packed up & marched southward all night, halted 15 minutes for rest, in the morning marched 2 miles & rolled up our sleeves and went into battle again.

Fought all the forenoon, gained nothing, & lost nothing but men. Fighting was in thick pine woods again, this was the 8th.

9th, heavy skirmishing all day, rebel sharpshooter sends his compliments over here rather too often for comfort.

10th, Charged on the rebel earthworks this morning, our reg't got separated from the rest of the line & lay right under the reb works without support from either flank. Finally fell back to our old position.

12th, Gen. Hancock with 2nd Corp's charged on our left & captured 7,000 prisoners & 18 pieces of Artillery. We were ordered to charge, advanced [to] the woods, & lost good many men when the order was countermanded. Were in line of battle all night, firing as fast as we could. Marched all the night of the 13th to where we now are, the rebels are in front of us still. The loss of our reg in killed & wounded in the campaign so far is 148 men & 8 officers and 14 missing, both Lieutenants of my co are wounded & there are 10 men left in the co. On the whole I think Grant has outgeneralled Lee. We have seen some hard fighting, I tell you, & expect to have more of it before the campaign is ended. Mail goes out in 10 min & I must close. Excuse all mistakes, this is written in haste. Much love to all, same to yourself. Please write soon.

Your Affn'te Cousin, Henry C. Matrau

I thank God, cousin Rusha, that I am permitted to answer your letter myself, whether your next finds me as well remains to be seen.

a. Henry's account of the action seems to stop before the armies moved from the Spotsylvania area. It is possible the date was added some days after the letter was actually written.

b. Jerusha Owen Woodruff, a distant cousin

In line of battle near the Chickahominy

June 1st/64

Dear Father & Mother,

I will take this opportunity to write you a few lines to let you know I am still alive and well. This is the 28th day's fight of this campaign & not a day of this campaign has passed but some part of the army has been engaged. To show you with what success we have been blessed, we were 70 miles from Richmond when we started and now we are on the Peninsula & 13 miles from the rebel capital, just the distance from "our house to St Jo." You have read better accounts of the battles in the newspapers than I would be able to write, so I will not go into the particulars of the campaign. Our reg't has lost 170 men killed wounded & missing scince the campaign commenced so you can judge we have seen some pretty tough fighting. The fighting isnt done yet but [we have] got the rebels in their strong hold's. The man commanding our Division, Brig. Gen. Wadsworth, was killed in the 2nd days fight. Please write soon and tell me all the news.

Your Affn'te son, Henry C. Matrau

Camp near Petersburg Va June 26th/64

Dear Mother,

I received your kind and welcome letter of the 18th last night and was very glad to hear from home and also very sorry to hear that Frank had acted in so foolish a manner, for I regard it as the very worst step he could take. Scince I wrote to you last, we have had more hard marching and fighting and more of my comrades have laid down their lives on the altar of their country. You are probably acquainted with the moves of the Army as well if not better than we are so I wont give any detailed acct of our moves but merely a few particulars. We crossed the Chickahominy river, after an all night march, the morning of the 13th at long bridge. Marched around the edge of White Oak swamp all day & halted at 12 oclock midnight & laid down & slept till morning, when we again pulled out & marched till noon and halted near Charles City Court House, within sight of the James river. Crossed the river on Govnt steam transports the 16th, & marched off on the main road towards Petersburg. Marched all day and night and the morn of the 17th formed in line of battle and dug rifle pits on the left of the 2nd Corps. The rebels shelled us all day with a small iron battery. The morning of the 18th we moved forward in line out of our work's. The rebels had abandoned their first line of works, leaving only a skirmish line in them, which we drove off after a few shots. We crossed the Richmond & Norfolk Rail-Road & moved up on the left of it through thick timber. We were under a severe artillery fire all the while and lost a few men. We got our dinner at $1\frac{1}{2}$ o'clock on a small creek in the edge of a field.

At 2 oclock we got orders to make an assault on the rebel works. We moved up through the field on to a sort of knoll when the reb's opened on us with a terrific fire of canister, schrapnel shells, & solid shot from their batteries & musketry from their infantry. We then had orders to right face & march cooly the length of the Rebel works, our men falling killed & wounded in every direction. Our General[a] saw that we couldnt stand this long, so we made entrenchments on the hill top. Our reg't lost 50 men killed & wounded in 15 minutes in this disastrous & useless affair. We are now consolidated into 4 companies & there are 134 muskets in the regt. We laid in our trenches till last night we were relieved to get a chance to wash our clothes & clean up a little for we needed this very much. I got a letter [from] brother Morgan the 22nd in answer to one I wrote. He was well & getting along finely. He didnt say where he was but his letter was post marked Memphis Tenn. Tell brother Eddie to be a good boy, that I have got a Musket bullet a Johnnie Reb shot at me which I will bring home & give to him when I get home. I am very sorry Cousin Rusha is so sick & am afraid she wont be able to write me any more letters. Tell Father I would like to be at home & help him in his work, for I know he must need help very much. I must close. Much love to all & please write soon.

Your Affnte son, Henry Matrau

[At the top of the first page]: Tell sister Lucy she must learn all she can to be a good girl & mind father & mother.

[At the top of the third page]: Tell brother Levi if I were at home I would give him another snowballing.

a. It is not clear which general Henry refers to in the letter. Perhaps it was Lysander Cutler, the division commander, or Edward Bragg, newly promoted to brigadier general.

Chapter Six

Letters of July 25, 1864, to February 3, 1865

So FAR, the campaign of 1864 had cost the Iron Brigade 902 casualties. A more significant loss, however, was the detachment of the Second Wisconsin to duty as provost guards. It was the first of the original regiments to leave the brigade.[1] The rest of the men settled into life in the trenches around Petersburg with the booming of big guns from both sides as their constant companion.

Grant and Meade were performing a vital function in tying down Lee's army, freeing Sherman to carry out his assignment further south. Starting at Chattanooga, he had pushed the Confederates into Atlanta, and on September 2 he moved into the city.[2] Lincoln knew his reelection hopes depended on the army's success in the field. Although the Battle of the Wilderness was costing heavy casualties, secret societies had formed to encourage desertion and wild rumors swept the North. One claimed that Lincoln had refused a Confederate peace offer. After Admiral Farragut took Mobile in August and Sherman entered Atlanta, however, public opinion started to swing in the president's favor.[3]

The Petersburg siege wore on, and federal troops launched a series of attacks on the rail- and wagon roads to the southwest that were still open to Confederate supply trains. The Weldon

Railroad ran from Petersburg to Weldon, North Carolina, and on August 18, Warren's V Corps moved to destroy as much track as possible. Skirmishing with the defending Southern forces developed into a full-scale battle as reinforcements arrived from both armies. Lee retreated four days later when it became apparent further contact was futile, but by then each side had suffered heavy casualties. The operation is known by various names: Weldon Railroad, Globe Tavern, and Six-Mile House. Among the wounded was Henry's division commander, Lysander Cutler, who did not return to field command.[4]

The continuing losses and the expiration of enlistment terms for some regiments led to further condensation of old units of the Iron Brigade. The Fourth Division was merged into the other divisions of V Corps, Bragg's men joining General Samuel Crawford's Third Division and renumbered First Brigade. New Pennsylvania regiments were added to Bragg's command along with the remainder of the old Second Wisconsin, now called the Independent Battalion, Wisconsin Volunteers. Later, the Indiana regiments were consolidated and transferred to II Corps, which caused great bitterness and resentment. In fact, some of the men tried to rejoin their old comrades during the battle of Boydton Plank Road in October and had to be driven back to their new command at bayonet point.[5]

With the Weldon Railroad in Union hands, one vital line remained open to Petersburg. It was the South Side Railroad, which ran west from the city to Lynchburg. As it left town, the line lay only a few miles behind the outposts on Lee's right flank at Hatcher's Run. On September 30, General Meade started a thrust west to probe the enemy strength and attack their defensive positions.[6]

October 27, V Corps was among troops that advanced across Hatcher's Run to cut the rail line and the Boydton Road. They ran into heavy fighting and difficult terrain covered with dense undergrowth that hampered movement and communication. The next day they were pulled back when it became apparent that reinforcements and supplies could not be assured.[7]

The last action of the year began on December 7. The men again moved on the Weldon Railroad, this time to destroy track forty miles south of Petersburg. They completed the assignment before Confederate troops could arrive in force and returned to camp on the 11th, settling in for the winter.[8]

While the Army of the Potomac fenced with Lee at Petersburg, Sherman left Atlanta and moved across Georgia on his "March to the Sea." This daring maneuver was successful, and he entered Savannah in December, having destroyed everything that could be of use to the Confederacy along the way. He next swung north into South Carolina, pushing to join Grant.

Toward the end of January, 1865, Confederate president Jefferson Davis appointed three peace commissioners to meet informally with Lincoln. They contacted Grant at Petersburg, and by the time arrangements had been made for safe transport to Washington the army grapevine was at work. Thus, when the three men drove out of the besieged city, walked across no-man's-land between the Northern and Southern trenches and entered the ambulances Grant had waiting for them, lines of soldiers were watching and cheering. On February 3, they met with Lincoln and Secretary of State Seward, but the South was still demanding independence and no agreement was possible.[9]

* * *

Near Petersburg, Va. July 25/64

Dear Mother,

I received your kind letter of the 18th inst last night and was very glad to hear from home. Those stamps came through all right and are very acceptable, I assure you. I am well and in tip top spirits and intend to keep so as long as I am in the Army. When I don a citizen rig instead of the blue one I now wear, I suppose I will have a perfect right to have the blues, but the Army regulation's strictly forbid it here. We are still in our old position before Petersburg and nothing [is] going on but the everlasting cannonading and mortar shelling, which keeps up a continual roar both night and day. But we have become so accustomed to this sort o' thing that we dont mind it and sleep as sound at night with shells bursting around and over us as we would at home out of range or hearing of cannon or bombshells.

Well, I suppose Sherman is pretty close to Atlanta now. A despatch arrived at our Army Headquarters night before last that Sherman was where he could shell the city and that Atlanta was as good as taken, for it would be shortly. If Atlanta is taken it will be as great a loss to the reb's as it would to take Richmond. If we only had that 500,000 men (that the President has called for) in the field now we could wipe out this Rebellion by the 1st of January next but as it is they wont be available in the field before the spring campaign of /65, which will make the war last a year longer and cause the loss of 100,000 more lives than would be necessary to crush the thing at once, just because there are thousands of young men in the north that are either too cowardly or too selfish to shoulder a musket like a man and help fight for their native country. Well, it seems the rebel raid into Maryland has fizzled out of the little end of the horn.[a]

Our enterprising friend's the Johnnie Reb's just over the way had all sorts of rumours that Baltimore was taken & Washington burned but they are still as mice now & dont have much to say.

We had a heavy shower yesterday afternoon & it rained hard all last night. This has cooled off the atmosphere and ground so that the weather is quite comfortable to day. The big gun called the "Petersburg Express"[b] is only a few rod's from where I am writing and keeps belching away, occasionally throwing the shells directly over our heads. Well, I must close. Much love to all, please write soon.

From Your Affectionate Son, Henry C. Matrau

P.S. If you could send me a small package of letter paper & envelopes I would be very much obliged, as it is impossible to get any here.

a. A special fear had been raised by Jubel Early's raid up the Shenandoah Valley. After defeating a Union force near Frederick, Maryland, Early led his men to the outskirts of Washington on July 11, cutting off communication between the city and the rest of the North. President Lincoln watched the severe skirmishing from the parapet of Fort Stevens on the 7th Street Road. As reinforcements arrived to help the defenders, the rebels withdrew into the valley, taking considerable loot with them. In response, Grant created the Middle Military Division and put Sheridan in charge, with orders to secure the Shenandoah Valley once and for all (see Boatner, 255–57, and Morison, 692).

b. The Petersburg Express (the Dictator), was a thirteen-inch seacoast mortar that had been mounted on a reinforced railroad car. When elevated at a 45-degree angle, it could throw a two-hundred-pound explosive shell 4,325 yards—about two and a half miles. Later, it was remounted in a fixed emplacement near Battery Four. See Boatner, 240, and Curt Johnson and Mark McLaughlin, *Civil War Battles* (New York: Fairfax, 1977), 146.

Camp near Petersburg Va

July 31st 1864

Dear Father and Mother,

As we have had another small burning of gunpowder, I will improve the opportunity of the first day of quiet in camp that we have had for over two months in writing you a letter describing something of the events that have happened in the last few days, of which you will probably get full details by the newspapers before this reaches you. We had been preparing for a general engagement of Artillery for the past three weeks; had made sunk forts of wicker baskets filled with dirt or rather sand, at short intervals along the front line, ready to place artillery in position and we dug roads wide enough for wagons with ammunition to pass in safe from the enemy's shell. More than this, the rebs had a large fort in front of Burnsides Corp's that "our folks" had undermined and placed a large quantity [of] powder under preparatory to send a few of the *Johnnies* with their cannon, &c, on an aerial voyage to the upper regions. Well, the night of [the] 29th everything was in readiness to blow up the fort and we moved up into the trenches about ten o'clock & formed in the 2nd line. We had orders to go to sleep and be ready to jump up under arms at three o'clock in the morning, for then the signal gun would fire, at which the fort would be blown up and our whole artillery open.

I didn't get asleep till 12 o'clock, the artillery was coming up and getting into position and the rumbling of the carriages & caisson's kept me awake. I was thinking too that we would in all probability make an assault of the enemies works in the morning and was turning over in my mind the possibilities & chances of my going through the melee unhurt or else getting a furlough to a better land. But nevertheless I finally fell into a sound sleep and was awakened in the morning by the explosion of the mine under the fort, which just made the earth tremble and started every man to his feet instanter. This was the signal at which the whole artillery and mortar batteries opened. To give you an idea of the noise we had, I will tell you the number of guns, &c, we had in the line of our brigade alone. There were 12 mortars, 24 pounder's, 12 brass 12 pound Napoleon guns,[a] 6 iron, 10 pound rifled guns, and seven 32 pounder rifled siege guns in the rear of us that threw shell's directly over our heads, besides big Cohorn iron mortars[b] on each flank.

It was the grandest sight I ever witnessed and the biggest noise too. I did'nt see the fort go up, I was'nt awake quick enough, but those who did said it looked like a powder blast on a pretty big scale. I understand it sent a battery with its complement of men and three companies to kingdom come. This took the rebs by surprise; they were having their morning doze, when men sleep the soundest, & the sudden concussion with the shrieking & howling of a thousand shells rather stupefied them with wonder.

A division of Burnsides were ready & rushed into the ruins of the rebel fort, took possession, & planted the old flag on the biggest heap of sand that was left. They went to work, carried sand bag's & made temporary works in the form of a half circle, for the rebs were still in their trenches on each side of them. It was clear they would'nt allow their lines to be broken this way if they could help it. Well, they made three seperate charges in the forenoon to recover lost ground but still our men held their own & captured many prisoners each time. So the day wore [on] apace. Our men could'nt gain any more ground, for the enemy had heavy batteries & forts on the heights above the town that could sweep the ground should a column of our men leave their cover. 2 o'clock in the afternoon, the rebels came down on this handful of men in the old fort in such masses that they drove them back & recaptured their fort and a good many prisoners.[c] This ended the fighting with our part of the line, what the rest of the army did we know nothing of yet, nor either our losses in killed, wounded, & prisoners. My reg't had three men only killed & wounded. We did'nt leave our works but supported the artillery. In the evening we were relieved & went back in the woods to our old camp & last night we marched off to the left flank of the army (ie) our brig. to do picket duty. We are in camp to day & every thing is quiet. Our men sent a flag of truce yesterday asking leave to bury our dead [and] take care of the wounded that lay on the ground, unable to get off. They could only get a truce of 15 minutes to put shades over the poor fellows to keep off the glaring sun & had to leave them there laying on the ground. The Johnnies gave them water, we could see them. I must close. Please write soon.

Your Affectionate Son, Henry Matrau

a. A Napoleon gun was a muzzle-loading, smooth brass field gun, very effective with canister or exploding shells, originally used by the French during the time of Napoleon III (see Boatner, 578).
b. Coehorn mortars were short-barrelled siege guns of various sizes used to lob explosive shells, invented by the Dutch engineer Baron Menno Van Coehorn. See Boatner, 161–62, and Ivan V. Hogg, *Fortress: A History of Military Defense* (New York: St. Martin's Press, 1975), 66.
c. Grant did not have enough personnel to carry out a successful assault on the enemy line, and the one serious attempt to dig tunnels and set off dynamite charges ended in the disaster of the crater on July 30. The explosion took the occupants of the Confederate fort by surprise and caused almost three hundred casualties. Federal troops swarmed into

the resulting crater and the field officers seemed to lose control of the situation. More and more soldiers entered and none was able to climb out the other side. The rebels regrouped and started firing into the pit. Worse yet, Confederate artillery found the range. The result was a casualty count of about four thousand killed, wounded, and captured, many of them Negro soldiers (see Boatner, 647–49, and Catton, *A Stillness at Appomattox*, 235–53).

Camp near Petersburg Va

Aug 8th/64

Dear Father & Mother,

Everything being quiet in camp this afternoon, I will scribble a few lines to let you know I am well as usual.

We are now encamped near the Petersburg & Norfolk R R on the extreme left of the Army.

There are no Rebs within 5 miles on our front. Our Division is doing picket duty, half of it being on picket all of the time while the other is in camp. Reliefs go out every two day's and it takes every man in camp to make the relief except the orderly Serg'ts of the several companies. Scince I wrote last to you I have been appointed Orderly Serg't.[a] I have a big company, too. One Lieut., 2 privates, & one Sergt comprises all that remains for duty in Co G, which formerly had an aggregate of over 100 men.

This will show you something of what the ravages of war are. A steady bombardment is kept up in front of Petersburg all of the time and our men and the reb's are busy mining and countermining. Our folks discovered one mine the rebs had dug under one of our batteries and they pulled out about 1000 lbs of powder deposited there for our benefit. Well, I suppose that the election fever is running high in B[ainbridge] now. Well, I hope it will turn out right in the end. I'll bet there are some sore heads about that 500,000 more men called for and prehaps Bainbridge has her share. As far as I am concerned, I only blame the President for not calling them out last winter. Well, mother, the principal object of my letter is to ask you if you will send me a couple of summer shirts.

We cant draw any but thick coarse cotton & wool shirts, & the weather is so excessively hot that they are rather uncomfortable. I would like them a little mixed with wool and of some plain color but not white. You can send them by mail by doing them up in a small compact bundle. Anything not exceeding 4 lbs in weight is allowed to come by mail to soldiers.

Well, I must bring this to a close. Tell Eddie & Levi & Lucy to be good boy's. We have not been paid in 5 months and probably wont get any for a month more at least. Much love to all.

From Your Affectionate Son, Harry

P.S. Father you must keep "*old Jack*" in prime order for I shall want to use him next winter, although I expect he would look forward to that event rather ruefully, thinking of the moonlight nights he would be kept trotting.

Harry

a. Orderly sergeant is the modern first sergeant, the chief enlisted assistant to a company commander. Henry's promotion came on August 1, 1864. (See Pension and Military Records of Henry C. Matrau, NARS.)

Near Petersburg Va Aug 15th 1864

My Dear Mother,

I received you[r] letter of the 8th inst last night and the writing paper and envelopes also. I am still in the enjoyment of good health but very sorry to hear that brother Morgan was sick.

I hope that the next news from him will tell of his recovery.

His disease is a very common one in the Army and there is hardly a man in the service but has had a turn at it, getting acclimated to the country and used to the soldiers style of living. I think that with the care of a good Surgeon he will get well. There has been nothing worthy of note going on here scince I wrote my last, except the usual shelling and digging.

We got paid 3 days ago and I have just put sixty dollars in the hands of the Chaplain of the 7th Wis.

He is going to City Point[a] to express a large am't of money for our brigade and mine will be sent by express with the rest. I have directed it to be sent as usual to St Joseph in care of B. C. Hoyt Esq. When you write, if you have heard anything from brother Morgan I wish that you would tell me, for I am very anxious to hear. Well, I must close as it is beginning to rain. Please write soon. Give my love to the children and the rest of the family.

From Your Aff'nte Son, Harry

a. City Point was a small hamlet near the present site of Hopewell, Virginia. The Union Army converted the town into a booming port connected with the troops by a railroad 21 miles long. (See Catton, *A Stillness at Appomattox*, 321–22.)

Near Petersburg Va Aug 17th

Dear Parents,

I write this to tell you that I have expressed twenty dollars more to day. I directed it in care of B. C. Hoyt as usual. This will make eighty (80) dolls I have sent to you this pay day and for fear that my other may not get through, I will tell you that I gave the chaplain of the 7th Wis sixty (60) dolls to take to City Point and express also. My pay this time amounted to $124.00.

Well, I am well as usual & must close.

Excuse haste,
Your Affnte Son,
H. C. Matrau

Near Petersburg Va Aug 27th/64

Dear Father and Mother,

I take this opportunity to tell you that we had another battle, or, rather, series of battles, scince I wrote last to you and that your unworthy son, by the watchful guidance of Providence, is still left alive and well.

I will not go into a regular detailed acct of the battles for I hav'nt the room or time. We left our camp in front of Petersburg the 18th inst and marched off towards the Petersburg and Welden Railroad, which we reached at noon and halted for dinner. The rebels attacked us with great fury about one P.M. but we held our own & repulsed them.

Our regt was deployed as skirmishers in front of our division and therefore lost very heavily.

The morning of the 19th our whole brigade was again deployed as skirmishers in front of a portion of the 9th Army Corps and a mile and a half from the main body.

The rebels again attacked us in the afternoon and we were obliged to fall back as fast as possible or be all taken prisoners. Our regt again lost heavily in killed and wounded. The only remaining Officer of my company, Lieut. John Timmons,[a] was shot through the body and killed instantly. Our Serg't Major[b] was killed. Capt. Hutchins[c] of Co B also met his death on that, to me, memorable afternoon.

When night closed the engagement, our men had retaken all that had been lost. On Sunday the 21st the rebels again attacked us and were again repulsed. The old sixth Wis has been terribly decimated in these fights and we now number 75 men, rank and file, in the reg't. When you write please let me know if you have rec'd that money or not, also please send some stamps. Excuse haste. Love to all.

Your Affnte Son, Henry

a. Lt. Timmons's enlistment had expired and he was waiting for the muster officer to arrive when the Sixth Wisconsin was ordered to march to Weldon Railroad. He decided to move with the regiment rather than remain in camp and was killed on the second day of the battle (see Dawes, 305, 309, 310).
b. The sergeant major was a man named Babcock. He died when a bullet hit the limb of a tree above him, was deflected downward, and struck him on the top of the head (see Dawes, 310).
c. William Hutchins had started as a corporal in Company B. He was leading his men as captain for the first time when he was killed (Dawes, 305, 307, 310).

Yellow House Va Sept 14th/64

Dear Mother,

Yours of the 29th Aug I rec'd a few days ago. I was glad to hear from home and to hear the money all got through safe. When I sent it, we were expecting a big fight soon and I didn't want to go into one with any money about me, for then I knew it was'nt at all certain whether old Hank would survive the battle or not. But a kind Providence did preserve me through it all right. There were many who were not so lucky, however, and many a poor fellow lost his life fighting for this Weldon railroad.

Well I suppose that between politics and the draft [the] country is in a state of continual excitement. Politics dont trouble us here in the Army much. The most we think about is whether the rebellion can be put down or not. I am satisfied that it can if the men that are needed only come out promptly.

Ulysses say's if old Abe will give him 100,000 more men he will take Richmond and end the Confederacy in 60 days. And he can do it.

Mother, when you write please send me a twenty dollar treasury note as I need it for immediate use. Please send it as soon as possible. Well, I must close. Please write soon. Much love to all.

Your Affectionate Son, H. C. Matrau

In line of battle near Yellow House Va

Oct 2nd 1864

My dear Mother,

I received your kind letter of the 23d ult this morning and the money was in it all right.

I didn't think we were going to get paid when I sent for that money but we were paid two months pay about a week ago. Scince I wrote last, the army has made a big move and part of it has been engaged in another big battle out near the South Side R R. We are now in line of battle to the left of the Yellow House & between the Weldon and the South Side rail road's but have not been engaged in battle yet. Our men met with some success on our left and captured a big fort and two lines of fortifications, one piece of artillery, and some prisoners. I believe they are not across the other road yet but are so near it as to command the RR with our artillery, so it is impossible to run trains on it now.

I am glad you told me where Morgan was, for I did'nt know where he was. I am glad he has got in the artillery, for it will be a great deal easier for him there.

I am sorry Uncle Mitchel[a] was drafted but Cousin Merrit[b] I think could very well afford to help defend our country, especially with the war so near a crisis as it is now. Any young man who is drafted now and forgets his manhood so far as to hire a substitute is'nt worthy the name of man and ought to be put in petticoats immediately.

Skirmishing is going on in our front all of the time I have been writing. We are in such a position now that the rebs will probably be obliged to attack us and we are looking for one every minute. But let them come, we are ready to send them back faster than they came. I suppose you think from my prescripts that I live in a yellow house. I dont, although Maj. General Warren commanding our Corps does. This Yellow House is an old yellow brick Tavern and from time immemorial has been known as the Yellow House.[c] It is now used as Corps Head Quartrs.

We have been having a cold fall rain and we are all nearly as moist as drowned rats. Well, Mother, I must close. Much love to all the family & reserve a big share for yourself. Please write soon. Excuse this miserable scrawl, for I have written in an awful hurry.

I remain
Your Affectionate Son,
Henry C. Matrau

a. Joseph's brother Mitchell Matrau
b. MaGloire Matrau, who used the name Merritt, son of Joseph's brother Peter
c. Yellow House was also known as Globe Tavern.

Yellow House Va Oct 30th/64

My Dear Parents,

I will take this opportunity to write you a few lines to let you know that your son is alive and well and never forgets his kind Father and Mother. When you wrote last, you said that brother Frank had gone to Kalamazoo & you were afraid that he would enlist. Scince then I have heard that he has enlisted. I am sorry he has been so foolish, for I think that he was needed at home.[a] It may be the best thing for him that he could do, for soldiering teaches one hard lessons, but they will last a man his life time. Scince I wrote last to you we have had another move but owing to some very blundering General were unsuccessfull. The morning of the 27th we broke camp, left our old earth works, & marched off to the left towards the South Side R R, about 7 miles, when we formed line of battle & moved through the woods. It was a real Virginia forrest of the densest description of small pines and a tangled mass of undergrowth, briars, & weeds. We got completely lost & bewildered in this jungle. The 2nd Corps ran into an ambush & were put to rout & the next morning, after a 24 hours campaign, we fell back to our old works. We are now encamped in precisely the same place that we were in before the move took place,[b] Scince I wrote last to you I have advanced another step in the line of promotion. I have received my commission as 1st Lieutenant of Co G and am now commanding officer of the company. You see, my father and mother, that I have arisen step by step to my present position as an officer in the U.S. Army. It has been by my own efforts, too, for I belong to a strange reg't from a strange state and the friend's I have now in the reg't I have gained scince the war began. I am rather proud, more for your sakes than my own, that I am able to present so clear a record of my services and I believe that my Parents will be proud of their son.

I dont wish to be thought any egotistical in thus speaking of myself but there ain't many that know how hard it is for a private to rise, as I have, from the lowest rank in the army to that of a commissioned Officer, with no help but my own right hand. My papers have gone to Division Hd Quarters & I will probably be mustered to morrow. I need some more money to enable me to get a respectable outfit such as a sword and belt, Officers uniform, &c, &c. I wish to make as respectable appearance as possible and my clothes are rather seedy now. I ought to have $30.00 and I would like to have you send me some at any rate, but dont send it by express but the same way you did the other, by mail. If you can spare me twenty dollars it will help me a great deal & when I get my Lieutenants pay I can easily refund it & more too. If the reg't is filled up with recruits I will be Captain of Co G.[c]

[At top of first page] Please send that as soon as possible. Give my love to all of the children & reserve a big share for Father & Mother. Kiss Lucy for me & tell her to be a good little girl. I must bring this to a close.

> I am as ever
> Your Affectionate Son,
> Lieut. H. C. Matrau

a. Frank Matrau was mustered into Company E of the 28th Michigan Infantry on September 30, 1864.

b. These encounters each cost lives and equipment and may have seemed futile to the men involved. The Union Army could replace its losses, however, and the Confederates could not, and after each skirmish the Union position was slightly improved (see Catton, *A Stillness at Appomattox*, 320).

c. This was Henry's first action as an officer, having received his first lieutenant's commission on the opening day of the battle. (According to the Records and Pension Office, it actually took effect on October 19, the date Lieutenant James Converse died.) His hopes for a quick promotion to captain of Company G did not materialize, however, because it was absorbed by Company D in November. (See Pension and Military Records of Henry C. Matrau, NARS.)

Yellow House Va Nov 17th 1864

Dear Mother,

Your kind letter with the $30.00 enclosed came through all right. I didn't like to send for that money but I could see no way to avoid, unless I either went without it or borrowed from men in the reg't, which I did not like to do. I thank you, father & mother, very much for this and many other favors, which I know I can never sufficiently repay.

My health is as good as usual. We have been having very pleasant weather for the past three or four weeks: but last night a cold fall rain set in.

It rained all night and is raining now, about as hard as it can pour down. We are in such comfortable quarters now that it seems rather pleasant to sit by a roaring old fire and listen to the merciless pelting of the storm outside: thinking too how many such storms we have weathered without even a rubber blanket to keep out the damp.

Well, the election is past & gone & I suppose that old Abe has a large majority.[a] We had a regular election here in the army. Our reg't went some 130 majority for Lincoln. Some companies did not cast a vote for Mac.

My company was very nearly even[ly] balanced. Four voted for Mac & 5 for Lincoln. I put in a straight Republican ticket myself. I thought I had served my Uncle Samuel long enough to entitle me to have a word to say about who is to run the machine.

I am glad that uncle Newton has been elected to the legislature, for I think that he is deserving of it & I dont know of another man in the town of B[ainbridge] more qualified to fulfill the duties of that office.[b] I have'nt had a letter from brother Morgan in a long while & I cant imagine the reason that he dont write. I shall write to Frank just as soon as I find time. I am glad that father has bought that place of Wat's.[c]

If God spares my life the ensuing year, I will send him money enough to finish paying for it and more too I hope. It is hard to tell whether we will be allowed to occupy our present comfortable quarters or not. I presume, though, that we will be obliged to leave them before the winter season is over. I dont know whether it will be possible for me to get a furlough this winter. Whenever they commence granting furlough's I shall apply for one, for I am as anxious to have a good visit with you once more as you are to see me. Tell little brother Eddy to be a good boy & when Christmas eve comes, may-be I will be old Santa Claus & put something nice in his stocking. Kiss Levi & Lucy for me & give my love to all the family. Please write soon.

> I remain
> Your affectionate son,
> Henry C. Matrau

a. Lincoln and his vice-presidential candidate, Andrew Johnson, won with 212 electoral votes against McClellan's 21, although the popular vote was closer (see Morison, 695).

b. Henry's uncle Newton Woodruff was elected to the Michigan state legislature and served one term. See *Portrait and Biographical Record of Berrien and Cass Counties, Michigan* (Chicago: Biographical Publishing Co., 1893), 374, under heading "Asaph Woodruff." See also Orville W.

Coolidge, *A 20th Century History of Berrien County* (Chicago and New York: Lewis Publishing Company, 1906), 245.

c. On November 9, 1864, Joseph bought forty acres in Section 14 from Waterman Young for one thousand dollars. (Berrien Township Register of Deeds, Michigan. Copy of deed to author, 26 August 1991.)

Camp near Petersburg Va Jan 15th 1865

Dear Mother,

I take this opportunity to write you just a few lines & in a terrible hurry. I am in good health & spirits, as usual, but I am going to try to get a furlough if possible & come home. We have'nt been paid off yet and if I get a furlough I shall need 40 dollars to pay my transportation north. If you will send me the money & send it with the letter in this envelope which I have backed & enclosed, I think I can get a twenty day furlough & come home. To get a furlough, a person has to have some near relative dangerously ill. So I wish you to take the enclosed envelope and put it in the P. O. at St Joseph & send it to me. When we make application for a furlough we have to send a letter with the application which we have rec'd telling of the death or sickness of wife, parents, or brother, or sister. Now when you send back this enclosed envelope you can put a letter in it & the money if you choose & write what you please, for I will use only the envelope. I will write, or get somebody to write, a letter stating that my wife Mary, Jane, Sally, or Polly are very sick & not expected to live, and put it in the envelope & send it to Army Head Quarters with the application for furlough. I don't like to resort to such means to get a furlough but I have to do it or else see all the rest going & stay like a gopher down here in Virginia till the spring Campaign opens. Please write soon as possible so I can put the thing through next week. Much love to all. I remain

Your Affectionate Son, Henry C. Matrau

Camp near Petersburg Va Feb 3d/65

My Dear Mother,

Your welcome letter of the 25th inst arrived by this morn-ing['s] mail and found me as well as usual. We are still occupying our winter qr's and enjoying life as much as is possible for a soldier to. I wrote a letter to you, I think it was on the 22nd January, but you said nothing about receiving it. I wrote for some money then. I dont like to send for money so often but we are all anxiously looking for the paymaster to make his ap-pearance. There are nearly 6 months pay due us now. I have got my application for a twenty days leave of absence on file at our regimental Head Quarters and as soon as one of the Officers now absent returns, it will be sent to Corps Hd Quarters for approval.

Still, I dont want you to make any great preparations, for something might happen that would prevent me going home. If Uncle Newton is only successfull in getting me that position, I shall be a thousand times obliged to him, for it will open to me a much larger field of action. Would'nt a petition to the Gover-nor [Henry H. Crapo], signed by all of the leading men of Berrien County, induce the Governor to favor the proposition? By the way, I must not forget to tell you that I received a letter from Brother Frank yesterday. His regiment has been trans-ferred all of the way from Nashville by rail to Alexandria, Vir-ginia. You may judge how surprised I was to learn that he was in Alexandria & only about 80 miles from here. Frank say's that they had an awful long journey & that most of his regt is sick & in Hospitals on the route but he say's (using his own expression) "I am tough as a bear." Alexandria is just across the Potomac river from Washington D.C. and about six miles from that city. Their regiment was stopping at the soldiers rest when he wrote & awaiting transports to go somewhere, he supposed to join Sherman. But I think in all probability that his reg't will be ordered to the city of Wilmington N.C.[a] There are all sorts of exaggerated rumors about peace going the rounds of the army. Still, we soldiers take them for what they are worth. I think however that the war is very near a close. I would like very much to go to Alexandria & see Frank but he might be away before I could get there. My great hope is now that Uncle Newton will succeed in getting me appointed to the West Point Military School as Cadet, for you cant imagine how much brighter prospects it will give me for future advancement in life. When you write, please tell whether you ever rec'd that letter that I wrote. I will in future direct my letters to Watervliet, as I think you will get them quicker than formerly. Well, I must close. Give my love to Father & Levi, Eddy & Lucy and please write soon.

As ever Your Affectionate Son,

> Henry C. Matrau
> 1st Lieut Co D 6th Wis
> Sixth Wis. Vet. Vols.

a. Combined naval and land forces attacked Wilmington, North Carolina, the last major seaport open to Confederate blockade runners. On January 15, Fort Fisher surrendered and on February 22, federal troops under General Jacob Cox finally entered the city (see Boatner, 293–94, and Bowman, 245, 251, 252).

Chapter Seven

Letters of February 13, 1865, to July 23, 1865

THE FIRST action of 1865 was the Battle of Hatcher's Run, or Dabney's Mills, a continuation of the moves to the southwest side of Petersburg that had started the previous year. It lasted from February 5 through 7 and cost heavy casualties. Henry's regiment was in the heaviest fighting but performed well, and this time the Union forces carried the field and did not pull back at the end of the engagement. Instead, they dug more trenches, thus extending their line.[1] They then settled back into the routine of a siege camp while awaiting further developments.

On February 10, Grant ordered Meade to send some reliable but reduced old units to Baltimore to take charge of camps for draftees. Meade ordered the First Brigade to go but Crawford objected, stating that he had many units that he could more easily spare. The Sixth and Seventh Wisconsin stayed at Petersburg as a result of his protest but the Twenty-fourth Michigan, which had been a part of the Iron Brigade since 1862, accompanied three Pennsylvania regiments to the north. A month later, a New York regiment joined the brigade and this, plus new draftees, brought its strength to over three thousand men.[2] The constant reorganization of units continued to cause morale problems among the men who were transferred and those who remained.[3]

By the end of March, heavy federal pressure had extended the line further left, almost completely surrounding Petersburg. When the siege began, the two armies had been roughly the same size, but now Grant outnumbered Lee approximately 115,000 to 54,000.[4] The Confederates made a desperate last stand at Five Forks, a crossroads southwest of town that they needed to retain control of the South Side Railroad and a hope of joining forces with Johnston's army. On March 29, Warren led the advance and met strong resistance at the Quaker Road crossing of Gravelly Run. His V Corps, including the Sixth Wisconsin, suffered 370 casualties.[5] The next day, General Sheridan, fresh from success in the Shenandoah Valley, took command of the operation.[6] In fierce fighting on March 31 and April 1, his men overran the Confederate breastworks, taking many prisoners. V Corps captured eleven flags and one gun but suffered 643 casualties.[7] The following day, a major assault on Petersburg by other elements of the Union army forced Lee to abandon that city and on April 3, federal troops entered Richmond.[8]

The remnants of the Army of Northern Virginia moved west, pursued by federal troops and unable to obtain food. Still, Lee hoped to join with General Johnston's army and perhaps reach Lynchburg and much-needed supplies. The retreat became a footrace. On April 8, Sheridan managed to place troops to the west of Lee on the Lynchburg Road. The next morning Lee attacked, but when it proved futile, he sent out a flag of truce. That afternoon, Grant and Lee met in the McLean farmhouse and signed the surrender documents.[9]

* * *

Bivouac in the woods near Petersburg Va

Feb 13th 1865

Dear Father and Mother,

Yours of the 27th January with the 40 dollars came through all safe. I should have answered it before this but we were on the move & fighting, so that I was obliged to wait until now.

I was glad to hear from home, you may imagine, but sorry to hear that my charming little woman was so feeble. Scince I wrote last to you we have made another move & had another fight.

We, (ie) the 5th Corps, left camp early in the morning of the 5th inst in light marching order, leaving tents, knapsacks and all superfluous baggage in camp with a detail of sick men to guard them. We marched off towards the South Side R R. Crossed Hatchers run in the afternoon, marched about 6 miles & halted about sunset. The 2nd Corps, on our right, then became engaged, and the canonading & musketry continued for one hour & a half. Something was up and we were ordered to fall in. We took the Boydton plank road & marched back towards Hatchers run where the 2nd Corps were fighting. We got there at day break in the morning and halted on what had been the battle field the evening previous. The 2nd Corps had driven the rebs from a line of hastily constructed rifle pits on the bank of the run and were in line of battle.

We made breakfast & stayed here untill 2 PM, when our Division, the 3d, marched out in front of the other troops, formed a line & advanced out through the woods to attack the enemy. We soon struck their skirmishers & comenced pressing them back. Pretty soon we struck their line of battle and then musketry and artillery opened in good earnest. We could get no artillery into position & therefore the rebs had a gay time cracking the spherical case and canister shot to us blue coats. Our regt did remarkably well considering that we had nearly 400 drafted men in the fight. Well, we had it backwards & forward, alternately driving the rebs & then getting [driven], our regt losing heavily all the time, on acct of being in an open field most of the time while the rebs were in thick woods. Finally, at about $4\frac{1}{2}$ oclock, our line to our left got broken & fell back in disorder. Our regt lay perfectly still and fired till our ammunition was completely exhausted & the rebels were getting around in our rear, when we fell back to the line of works the 2nd Corps had thrown up the night before. It now became dark & we were relieved by the first Division of our corps, which had not been engaged. We went back to the run & laid down for the night, pretty well worn out with the day's work. Capt. [John] Lammey of my Company was severely wounded in the head & I was left in command of the company. The Captain is now in Hospital at City Point, but his wound is of such a dangerous Character that it isnt thought by the Surgeon that he can recover. Well, to go on in my story. A cold Sleet & rain storm set in in the night and in the morning it was dreary & disagreeable enough I tell you.

Well, we were ordered to fall in at 9 oclock, we had done so well the day before & lost so many men that we were picked out to make another attack on the rebels, who were by this time behind good works. Well, we formed line again & lay in the woods under a severe fire of Artillery & a drenching cold rain till 3 PM, when we were pushed forward to the attack. We found their works on the opposite side of a ravine full of water. We had only one thin line of battle & so we halted by the ravine & fired away till we lost about 100 men in the Brigade, when we fell back to the works. We laid there 2 days, built works, made corduroy roads, &c, &c.[a]

We were then sent back to camp to get our things. We staid

in camp one night. In the morning, 1200 men of our Brigade were ordered to Baltimore & New York Cities for special duty.

Well, they took Pennsylvania regts & left our two Wisconsin regts, the 6th & 7th, to stay in the Army of the Potomac. Our Brigade is broken up and we have not been assigned to any particular command yet.

We are laying in the woods without tents or any shelter & dont know what the devil they will do with us. I suppose it will be impossible to get a furlough at present while every thing is so unsettled.

I hope, however, that Uncle Newton will not leave anything undone that will secure me that position. I would give any thing in the world to have it succeed. Please ask him not to leave a stone unturned & employ every means in his power to push the thing through.

He might get up a petition & get all of the prominent men in the County & State to sign it, that would probably do some good. Excuse this miserable scrawl for it is written on my knee by the side of an awful smoky fire & out of doors to[o]. The weather is so cold I have to stop every 5 minutes to warm my fingers. Please write soon. Much love to all. In haste from

Yr Affnte Son, Henry C. Matrau

P S The loss in our regiment in the 2 fights is 175 killed wounded & missing.

a. Corduroy roads were used in backwoods areas where a new road was needed quickly. Logs were laid across the roadway to keep wheels from sinking into the mud. The wagon, therefore, bumped across each log in turn, making for a very rough ride. More refined plank roads were built also, the heavy planks being spiked to parallel stringers. They were reasonable when new but soon degenerated as the wood split and rotted. See J. C. Furnas, *The Americans: A Social History of the United States, 1587–1914* (New York: Charles Scribner & Sons, 1984), 278, 279.

Camp near Petersburg, Va. Feb 22nd/65

My Dear Mother,

Your kind letter of the 14th and 15th insts came to hand today & I will improve the present opportunity of scribbling an answer. I am very thankful that my relatives and friends are taking so much interest in my behalf & I sincerely hope that their efforts will be *very* successful, for it seems to me that it is my surest and only true way to open before me a path to a wider field of usefulness in life. I dont know how it will be now about me getting that leave of absence, every thing is so unsettled and therefore I would like to have Uncle Newton use his utmost endeavors to put my project into execution if he can. Prehaps it will be in my power to repay some of my very many debts of gratitude to my relatives and friends in some future time, (ie), if Providence spares my life through the war.

We are now busy putting up winter quarters again. It seems as if our 5th Corps has more houses to build than any Corps in the army. The reason of this is we are the best Corps in the army & when they have any difficult job to perform they always select our Corps & Maj Gen Warren to do it. Consequently we do not remain in one place more than 3 weeks at a time. We are now to the left & east of the Weldon R R and about one mile from Hatchers Run. I have got my shanty almost built. Three men in my company, good, handy fellows, are making it and it will be about the nicest house in the regiment. I received official notice this morning that the Captain of my Company, John R. Lammey, was dead. He died in our field Hospital at City Point, Va.

He was wounded the 6th of Feb on Hatchers Run, in the head, and lived 10 days. The command of the Company now devolves upon me. I have quite a large Company now, & with a large number of wounded in the last fight it keeps me pretty busy making out descriptive lists, &c. I received that $40.00 all safe. An order has come to regt'l Hd Qr's not to muster for pay untill we have been paid what we are already mustered for & it is pretty certain that the Paymaster will make his appearance soon. No troops will be more pleased to see him than ourselves for greenbacks have had a very limited circulation with us for the past two months. I have'nt heard from Brother Frank scince he wrote that letter from Alexandria. I think that they are in South Carolina by this time.

If it is possible for me to get a leave of absence, rest assured I shall get out & I shall see the Governor, also, if possible. But I think Uncle Newton can do more than I can to influence the Governor, for the Governor will hardly see enough to interest his favor in a young, weather beaten, tanned, old veteran of four years hard marching and fighting.

Nevertheless I will hope and pray for the best and always endeavor to look on the bright side. Well, Mother, I have written more now than you will have patience to read so I will close with much love the Father, Mother, brothers, and sisters.

From Your ever Affectionate Son,

Henry C. Matrau

Camp near Petersburg Virginia

March 23d 1865

Dear Father & Mother,

I arrived safe in camp on the 21st inst & found my regt just where I left them and every thing quiet along the lines, although we are prepared to move in any direction & have sent all surplus baggage to the rear. I was delayed on the Rail Road in Pa on acct of freshets & high water. when I got to Harrisburg I found that 8 miles of the track between there & Baltimore was submerged in water & no trains were running through. So that evening I went to Philadelphia. I got in Philadelphia early Sunday morning & of course had to stay untill the next mornings as no cars run on the Sabbath. I attended church twice while there & visited the City Park and reservoir. Monday morning I came on to Baltimore and left Baltimore for Fort Monroe on the U.S. mail boat in the evening. I arrived at City Point the next day & got to my regt in the evening. I found my Captain's commission here ready for me. I was mustered as Captain yesterday.[a] The boys were all glad to see me and I was glad to see them, for I was tired of rail-roading. Tell Cousin Rose & Aunt Sarah that honey they sent got out of the can by rough handling on the cars & some of it got where I least wanted it, (ie), mixed up with the things in my valise. But there was enough left to give the boy's a good taste and they all wish me to send their best respects to Uncle A[saph], Aunt Sarah & Cousin Rose.

The news here is good. Sherman keeps marching on & baffles all efforts of the rebels to stop him. He captures every town in his way & sometimes goes a little out of his course to take a place. Sheridan is at White House on the Pamunkey river & within almost speaking distance of our army. We are here & doing more than any other army in the United States ever has yet done, (ie), holding nine tenths, $\frac{9}{10}$, of the rebel army here and allowing the others to march wherever they choose with nothing to oppose them.

Tell me when you write whether Morrison has heard any thing further, definite, concerning my transfer to the regular

Service. Please send some Postage Stamps in your next. Well, [it] is after tattoo & I must close. My respects to all enquiring friends. My love to Levi, Lucy, & Eddy & the same to Father & Mother. Please write soon.

Your Affnte Son, Henry C. Matrau

Direct to
Capt H C Matrau
Co D 6th Wis Vet Vols
Ist Prov Brig, 3d Div. 5th A.C.
Washington D.C.

P S I send by this mail my Lieutenant's Commission. You will see that it came in contact with that everlasting honey. Please tell me in your next whether or not of its safe arrival.

H C M

a. Henry was promoted to captain on March 7 but received captain's pay retroactive to February 5, when he took command. (See Pension and Military Records of Henry C. Matrau, NARS.) According to his obituary in the *Norfolk Press* (Nebraska) of January 11, 1917, he "is said to have been the youngest captain in the United States Army."

Appomattox court House Va

April 10th 1865

My Dear Father & Mother,

I write this to let you know that we have seen some hard fighting & marching & that I have been again spared the fate of many of our brave boys.

I suppose you will hear, before this reaches you, that Petersburg & Richmond have both fallen into our hands & the starry banner floats over the once Capital of the Southern Confederacy.

Blessings never come singly, for yesterday, Sunday the 9th April, Gen. Lee surrendered the whole rebel army under his command to us. The rebel army is now camped within $\frac{3}{4}$ of a mile of us with their arms stacked. Yesterday was indeed a glorious day for us. We had their army surrounded, had captured nearly the whole of their wagons, commissary, Stores, & artillery, & were just preparing to attack them on 3 side[s]. Gen. Lee saw that it was useless to hold out longer, so he, like a sensible man, surrendered himself and his whole army. Gen. Grant & Lee are now together.

I dont know how many men there are in the army of Gen. Lee, but from where we can see them they look like a pretty big squad. They are mostly Virginia troops & will be allowed to go to their homes after taking the oath of allegiance to the U.S. I have'nt the time to tell you the particulars of our marching & fighting for the past two wks but suffice it to say we have done harder fighting than any other Corps in the army, although we did not see Petersburg or Richmond. Our first fight was March 31. We lost in our regt over 100 men. My Company lost 10 men killed & wounded. Apr 1st, we marched to the extreme left flank of the army & were then under command of Gen. Phil Sheridan.

We attacked the rebs in the afternoon with both Cavalry & infantry, drove them out of works, followed, & captured nearly the whole of one Corps & besides that we captured the South Side Rail Road. The next day we received the news that Petersburg was taken and the next day a dispatch came stating that Richmond was in possession of our forces. Has not April been to us a glorious month? Where are the men now who said that the army of the Potomac has never accomplished any thing? I have been very fortunate again. I think our hard fighting is over & the boys are beginning [to] plan what they will do for a living when the war is over.[a] Tell Levi, Eddy, & Lucy to be good boys, that Brother Hank will if he lives, be at home to stay a while pretty soon. This our first chance to send away mail. I must close, much love to all & please write soon.

Yr affectionate Son, Henry C. Matrau

a. The war continued for a short while after Appomattox. April 26, General Johnston surrendered to Sherman and on May 10, President Jefferson Davis was captured in Georgia. General Taylor surrendered all remaining forces east of the Mississippi and on May 26, General Buckner did the same for the west. The last Confederate flag to come down was on the CSS *Shenandoah*, which finally surrendered in England on November 6, 1865 (see Boatner, 441, and Morison, 701–2).

Camp near Burkeville, Va. Apr 18/65

Dear Mother,

Your letter of the 5th inst came to hand by yesterday's mail. I was glad to hear that the "folks at home" were all well. I wrote you a letter at Appomatox C H a few days ago, scince then we have marched about 65 miles back to Burkeville junction & are now camped about 6 miles from the junction. We are going to move about three miles tomorrow & go into a regular camp, where we probably shall stay for some time & recruit up. We need it bad enough I assure you.

I wish you could see me now, as I am writing under an old oak tree. You would think your son was a sorry looking object. I have waded creeks, plunged into swamps & morasses, laid in the dirt until I look more like a gopher than a human being. My photograph came a few days ago & I will send one in this letter.[a] It is getting dark & I havent time to write much this time. Give my love to Levi, Lucy, & Eddy, & all enquiring friends. Tell father I shall be at home & help him next winter. Please write soon.

> Your Affnte Son,
> H. C. Matrau
> Capt Co D 6 Wis

a. The photograph shows Henry in the dark blue frock coat of a Union Army officer.

> Apr 19/65

Dear Mother,

We havent yet moved & I couldnt get my letter posted yesterday so I will write a little more today. We have just got the news that President Lincoln has been murdered by a certain Booth of Washington.

Isnt that a burning shame? They didnt want him to live to enjoy the glory of having crushed the rebellion.

I was astonished to learn that Eugene Cribbs[a] had gone as a substitute. I shouldnt think his parents would allow that. He will never see much service, however, and will probably never see a fight. We soldiers think that the war is about ended and the boys are now making their calculations on what kind of business to engage in when peace is declared.

Well, I must close. Please write soon. Much love to all.

> Your Affectionate Son, Henry C. Matrau

a. The Cribbs family owned a farm in Bainbridge.

Camp near Alexandria Va May 14/65

Dear Mother,

Yours of the 1st inst was received yesterday. It found me alive & well after a fatiguing march of 200 miles from Blacks & Whites Sta on the South Side R R. We marched through Petersburg, the "Cockade City," that we were so long besieging.[a] From there we marched to Richmond. We camped for 3 days on the south side of the James River near the city of Manchester & within sight of the capital of the once so called Southern Confederacy. The 6th of May I obtained a pass & took a ramble through the City of Richmond. I visited Libby Prison, and found it full of rebel prisoners. It is a large, low, three story brick building with the upper story painted white & the lower two story's the red color of the brick. It was once an old Tobacco ware house. I also saw Castle Thunder, another "Bastile" of the rebellion. This is likewise a brick building with slate roofing. I saw the old U S Custom House, where the Rebel Congress conducted its deliberations, and also the residence of Jefferson Davis.[b] The rebels burned some of the largest and most costly buildings in the City. I suppose this was done in order that the Citizens of Richmond might have something to remember their *brave defenders* for.

In the evening I went to the Richmond Theater. The play was the French Spy.[c] The next morning we broke camp & march[ed] through the City of Richmond. We were reviewed by Gen's Meade and Halleck. We then took up the line of march towards Fredericksburg. We came in sight of Fredericksburg on the 8th & camped three miles from the town. The next morning early we resumed our line of march for Alexandria. Arrived here the 12th inst. We are camped now within sight of Washington. I cant tell when we will be discharged. They are busy now discharging men in Hospitals.

It seems strange that Frank dont write, but I should'nt wonder if I could guess the reason. I presume he has either obtained a furlough or his discharge & he probably wishes to surprise you some of these fine days.

I have not seen Eugene yet. I am kept so busy now making returns, Descriptive Lists, discharges, &c, &c, that I hardly have time to eat my meals. The Division Eugene's regiment is in, is camped two miles from here. I shall hunt him up, however, just as soon as I possibly can. My health still remains good although I am pretty tired after our long continued marching. I am in hopes I can be with you in August. I could, I think, get out of the Service now by sending in my resignation, but I had rather remain untill my regiment is discharged. Tell Eddy to be a good boy, for brother Hank is coming. Much love to Father, Mother brothers & sister Lucy.

Your Affectionate Son, Henry C. Matrau

a. During the War of 1812, volunteer infantrymen from Petersburg wore black leather rosettes, or cockades, in their hats. The company distinguished itself during the defense of Fort Meigs on the Ohio River and was commended by President James Madison. He dubbed it the "Cockade City" and the title is still used today (letter to editor, May 23, 1989, Visitors' Bureau, Petersburg, Va.).
b. Libby was located on the James River. It was used to hold Union officers and was second only to Andersonville in notoriety. After nearby Union raids in 1864, the prisoners were sent further south to Macon, Georgia, and Libby became a temporary holding station (see Boatner, 482, and Francis T. Miller, ed., *Prisons and Hospitals: A Photographic History of the Civil War* (New York: Castle Books, 1957), 55, 56, 91, 93–95). Castle Thunder, also a converted warehouse, held political prisoners including those accused of treason or spying. Its officers were

rumored to use unnecessary brutality and force in controlling their charges. There was also another prison with this name in Petersburg (see Boatner, 131).

c. *The French Spy; or, The Siege of Constantina*, was a military drama in three acts. It was written by John Thomas Haines with music by Auber and was originally presented in Paris in 1830 (telephone conversation, May 25, 1989, staff of Mercer County Library, N.J.).

Head Quarters Co "D" 6th Wis Vet Vols

                      Near Alexandria Va June 6th 1865

Dear Father and Mother,

Your kind letter with the $50.00 enclosed came through all right. I thank you very much for your kindness and I assure you it arrived very opportunely. We are still encamped near Washington on the Virginia side of the Potomac. We had the grand review as laid down in the programme but I suppose you have read good accounts of the affair in the newspapers so I wont bother you with the particulars.[a] Troops are being sent home now every day but I dont think we will be discharged before fall, if we do then. When I wrote to you I was stopping in Washington and it was generally supposed then that we would be mustered out as soon as our accounts could be straitened & settled. Scince then an Order from the War Dept has been issued that no Veterans shall be discharged at present. They are sending home every day, now, men whose time expires before Oct 1st 1865. 74 men were mustered out of our regt, most of them drafted men who joined us last fall & some of them men who have never seen a battle or smelled gun powder. I think that the Gov't is not only injuring her own interests but doing great injustice to men who have been her only true support through four long weary years of a terrible conflict. I need not say that the "veterans," the men who perilled fortune, limb and life to sustain the republic, are extremely disatisfied. These men they are discharging now are men who should we become involved in another war would never volunteer to help their country even if an enemy should invade their own territory & lay waste their snug little farms & domicil's. But in six months, after they are discharged, these same men they are using so badly now will forget all this & enlist to help their country as willingly as they did in 1861. The Gov't may have some good object in view that we can not understand. I am confident that they do what they think is for the best. I hear that the report is now that western troop[s] will be sent to Louisville Ky, there to be discharged Vets & all. I hope it is true but there are so many rumours in circulation that one is safer in disbelieving all of them than crediting any. Board's of Examination have been appointed & met to examine officers who wished to remain in the service. A Circular came around directing all officers to make out a military history of themselves, (ie), state the number of battles in which engaged, length of time in the service, & date of promotions. Also to state whether the officer wished to remain in the service or not. As I did'nt wish to remain in the Volunteer service and I knew I could not pass a board of examination for the regular service I stated plainly on mine that I did not wish to remain in the service. I knew that although I can drill a Company & understand the tactics as well as any Volunteer officer in the service who has never had an opportunity to study & has learned everything by practice, that although I can get the commanding officer of my regiment to testify as to my ability to handle a company of men in battle, yet I could not pass examination from the fact that I have got the practice and not the theory. All of the officers in our regt except two were like my-self; they did'nt wish to remain in the service. So the board went to work and made a report to the War Dep't, reccommending such officers as they liked best to be kept & those they thought least deserving to be discharged. As near as I can ascertain I am one of those recommended to be kept in the service. Our Major, D. B. Dailey, who was one of the Board of Examination, is quite a friend of mine and as he wishes to remain in the service him-self, he probably would like to have me stay also. I dont see what is the reason that I dont hear anything more about that transfer to the regular Army. Well, prehaps it will be better for me if it does not succeed for then I could go to school when I *am* dis-charged & obtain an education that would fit me for any posi-tion in life or profession either. Still a position in the regular Army with the same rank I now hold would be worth something and I would not accept a Commission lower in grade than Cap-tain. My pay in time of peace would be no inconsiderable thing, about $170.00 per month, and then I probably would have a pretty good chance to improve my education. At present I am watching the tide of events as they float along. I shall continue to hope for the best & endeavor to improve every opportunity as well as I can. I am Officer of the day to day & will be obliged to close this to attend to my duties. I was sorry to hear that brother Frank had been so sick but I hope before this reaches you he will be at home again. My love to Levi, Lucy and Eddy, the same to Father & Mother.

Your Affectionate Son, Henry C. Matrau

a. On May 23, Pennsylvania Avenue in Washington was filled with men of the Army of the Potomac marching under the banners that had led them in battle. The remaining regiments of the old Iron Brigade pa-raded together in this grand review in a final show of pride. The records show that this brigade suffered a greater percentage of killed and mortally wounded men than any other in the Union Army (see McPherson, 528, and Nolan, 281–82). According to *Regimental Losses in the American Civil War* by William F. Fox, the Sixth Wisconsin lost 244 men killed in action or dying later of wounds, placing it tenth on the list of absolute loss and thirtieth in percentage lost (12.5 percent). The regiment also had 113 deaths from disease and accident or in prison (see Nolan, 381–82).

Camp near Jeffersonville Ind

June 30th 1865

Dear Father & Mother,

Scince I wrote last to you we have performed a journey of several hundred miles.

We broke camp near Alexandria Va the 16th inst & marched to Washington. We took the cars at the Baltimore & Ohio R R Depot & left there about 10 AM the same day. We passed the Relay House in the afternoon. Here the Rail Road turns to the left & proceeds on its way towards Va. We passed Harpers Ferry where we crossed the Potomac river at day-break the next morning. Our journey was continued by rail to Parkersburg, West Va on the Ohio river & was so nearly like all trips by rail that I wont give details.

We passed through a very mountainous region & tunnels innummerable. I think we passed through 23 tunnels. We arrived at Parkersburg, the end of the road, the 18th inst in the evening. Here we camped for the night just outside of the town. We embarked on Steamboats in the Ohio river the next day. Our "voyage" down the Ohio river was a very pleasant one, much pleasanter than riding on crowded cattle cars. We arrived in Louisville K'y the 21st inst [and] after laying in one of the principal thoroughfares of the town 3 or 4 hours, they finally concluded to put us into camp on the Indiana side of the river. We crossed on the ferry to Jeffersonville & went into camp about 2 miles from the town.

It seems rather strange to be camped in a Northern State & in Hoosierdom too. I dont know when they intend to muster us out of the service but I think we will be discharged in the course of two months at fartherest. Please tell me in your next if you have heard from Morgan & Frank lately & where they are. Our men are all greatly disatisfied about being kept in the service & some have commenced deserting.[a] Well I must close. Much love to all. Please write soon.

Your Affectionate son, Henry C. Matrau

Direct
Capt H.C. Matrau
Co D 6th Wis Vet Vols
Prov Div.A' of T'.
Louisville. Kentucky.

a. On June 20, the Sixth and Seventh Wisconsin and Twentieth Indiana (containing the remnants of the old Nineteenth, an original Iron Brigade regiment) reported to Louisville, Kentucky, and were incorporated into the newly formed provisional division of the Army of the Tennessee. In July they were mustered out of the service, one regiment at a time (see Nolan, 382). In spite of Henry's complaints about the slow demobilization of the army, it was reduced from 1 million men to 183,000 by November, 1865, and reached 25,000 by the end of 1866 (see Morison, 706–7).

Madison Wis July 23d 1865

Dear Father and Mother,

The first letter I wrote to you after I started on my soldier carreer was from this place, I believe, and now I think I am safe in saying that this, my last, is written in the same place. We left our camp at Jeffersonville, the 14th inst. The same day we were mustered out of the U.S. service and arrived here in Madison the 18th inst and went into the barracks at old Camp Randall.[a] The camp is much changed, although I dont find it hard to recognize the old well trodden beats around the camp that I used to perambulate with an old flint lock musket in my hands, thinking with a proud feeling of satisfaction, what a *man* I am and wont *I* make a brave soldier though. There have been many alterations scince we were here in /61. The old shed with its rows of board bunks filled with straw, where I lay two or three weeks with the measles, has been pulled down and more substantial barracks built instead. Nearly everything inside of the Camp is changed except the parade ground we used to have our squad drills on. We are waiting now to be paid off and get our final discharges. I have got my Company books & papers very nearly all finished. I have turned over all of my Camp & Garrison Equipage, Guns & accoutrements, & every species of public property of which I am responsible.

We expect to be paid next Thursday. You can expect to see me home if nothing happens within 12 or 14 days at fartherest. I shall start for home just as soon as I can get my pay & final discharge from the Government. Well, I must bring this scrawl to a close. Give my love to Levi, Eddie, & Lucy & keep a share for father and Mother.

Your Affectionate Son, H. C. Matrau

a. Henry was honorably discharged at Jeffersonville, Indiana, on July 14, 1865 (see Pension and Military Records of Henry C. Matrau, NARS). Two days later, the Sixth Wisconsin arrived in Madison and received a public welcome at the fairgrounds. The veterans performed a drill to the music of fife and drum and then disbanded to return to their homes (see Nolan, 382). In 1880, the Iron Brigade Association was organized, open to all soldiers and officers who had been honorably discharged. It was civil in nature, with enlisted men just as eligible for its elective offices as their wartime commanders. The membership fee was twenty-five cents (see Nolan, 383).

Epilogue

HENRY MATRAU did return to Watervliet, but his hopes for
a military career never materialized. On October 8, 1867, he
married his "Cousin Rusha," Jerusha Owen Woodruff, the
daughter of William Woodruff and Jerusha Owen Woodruff of
Three Rivers, Michigan.[1] Together they raised a family of five
children. After some years in Berrien County, the couple moved
from place to place in the Midwest, settling at last in Norfolk,
Nebraska, in 1884 or 1885. For the next twenty years, Henry
was the station agent for the Chicago and Northwestern Railroad.[2] He became active in community affairs, serving as secretary of the school board, mayor in 1893 and 1894, and was a
member of the state legislature for Madison County during
the 1911 session. He was a member of the Commercial Club;
the Mathewson Post of the Grand Army of the Republic; and
the Nebraska Commandery Loyal Legion, serving as its commander for one term.

After leaving the railroad in 1907, Henry ran a coal and
lumber business with Theodore Wille in Norfolk; six years later
he moved to Windsor, Colorado, to continue in the same business.[3] There he also continued his association with the Grand
Army of the Republic as a member of the Rutherford B. Hayes
Post. On January 5, 1917, he died while undergoing dental

surgery, and his body was sent to Lincoln, Nebraska, because most of his children were living near that city.[4] The Grand Army of the Republic conducted the burial service at Wyuka Cemetery and the *Norfolk Press* reported that the casket was covered with the Stars and Stripes and that there were many floral tributes.[5] A more lasting tribute to his many civic services can still be found in the city of Norfolk — Matrau Street.[6]

His parents remained on the family farm in Michigan. In 1873, they are listed as founding members of the Bainbridge Grange, Number 80. Their sons, Morgan and Edward, continued the family's farming interests until the arrival of daughter Lucy's husband, Will Cook, freed Edward to pursue a business career. In 1880, Joseph joined the Church of Christ, or Christian Church, and remained an active member until his death. Amanda died October 18, 1889, and Joseph, May 21, 1893.[7]

Henry's widow, Jerusha, disposed of the family business in Colorado and then made her home in Lincoln, Nebraska, with a daughter. She died March 20, 1928.[8]

Who's Who in Henry's Letters

Bragg, Edward S.
Edward Bragg was a lawyer from New York who moved to Wisconsin in 1850 and became active in Democratic party politics. He served as prosecuting attorney for Fond du Lac County and was a delegate to the 1860 Democratic convention. As an officer with the Sixth Wisconsin, Bragg was wounded at Antietam and while convalescing was nominated for Congress as an independent "war" candidate. He was defeated and returned to the army, eventually ending the war in Baltimore as a brigadier general. Bragg's political career continued and he served as a Democratic congressman, minister to Mexico, and consul general to Havana and then Hong Kong.[1]

Burnside, Ambrose E.
Ambrose Burnside was a businessman from Rhode Island and a graduate of West Point who had served in the Mexican and Indian wars. He reentered the army in 1861 as a colonel but quickly advanced to major general of volunteers. He twice refused command of the Army of the Potomac, feeling inadequate for such a position, but he accepted a third offer at the urging of fellow officers.[2]

Burnside was himself replaced by Hooker after his disastrous failure at Fredericksburg but remained in the service as commander of the Army of the Ohio. In 1864, Grant recalled him, and Burnside led the IX Corps through the battles of the Wilderness and on to Petersburg. There he mishandled troops during the Crater assault and was relieved by his chief of staff. He retired soon after.

Burnside's postwar career was more successful. He returned to business as an engineer and manager of several railroads and served three terms as governor of Rhode Island. At the time of his death in 1881 he was a U.S. senator.[3]

Cutler, Lysander

Lysander Cutler was born in Massachusetts but lived most of his life in Maine, where he engaged in various businesses, including a woolen mill, a grist mill, a sawmill, and a foundry. His success in business led to public office and he was a leading citizen until financially ruined by the panic of 1856.

Starting again in Milwaukee, Cutler worked for a mining company (a dangerous job that involved trips to Indian country to investigate claims) and eventually established his own highly successful grain business — in fact, he became a millionaire.[4] When the Civil War began, he volunteered, in spite of the fact that his only military experience had been the command of a militia in Maine during the Indian wars of 1838 and 1839. He was fifty-three when he was appointed colonel in command of the Sixth Wisconsin Regiment. He was wounded in the leg at the Battle of Brauner Farm (Gainesville) but returned to duty just as McClellan was replaced by Burnside. He was still crippled when he took to the field with his men at Fredericksburg. During the battle, General Meredith was temporarily relieved of command by his division commander and Cutler was in charge of the Iron Brigade during its well-executed rear-guard action at the Rappahannock River. Shortly thereafter, he was promoted to brigadier general in command of the Second Brigade.

Following Gettysburg, the old I Corps was absorbed by General Warren's V Corps, and Cutler assumed command of the survivors of the old Iron Brigade. At the Battle of the Wilderness, Wadsworth, the division commander, was killed and Cutler took his position. He was then wounded at Globe Tavern on August 21 and finished the war at draft rendezvous in New York and Michigan. He was breveted major general of volunteers and after Appomattox returned to private life. Cutler died in Milwaukee the following year.[5]

Dailey, Dennis B.

Although from Lebanon, Ohio, Dennis B. Dailey entered the army as a member of Company B of the Second Wisconsin. He advanced to the rank of major in December, 1864, and was named second-in-command of the Sixth. During the Battle of Five Forks, he was wounded while temporarily leading the 147th New York but later returned to assume command of the Sixth.[6]

Henry's contact with Dailey continued after the war, and when Dailey died in Council Bluffs, Iowa, March, 1898, Henry was one of the mourners at the funeral.[7]

Doubleday, Abner

New Yorker Abner Doubleday was educated as a civil engineer and worked at that profession for two years before entering West Point. Upon graduation, he served in the Mexican and Seminole wars and was stationed at Fort Sumter in 1861. As captain of artillery, he is said to have aimed the first gun fired in its defense.

Doubleday fought in the Shenandoah Valley, at the Second Battle of Bull Run, South Mountain, and Fredericksburg, rising to the rank of major general by November, 1862. When Reynolds was killed at Gettysburg, Doubleday successfully took over the corps and thus expected a promotion to corps command afterwards. He was passed over, however, and subsequently transferred to Washington, away from field service. The only action he saw during the remainder of the war was in defense of the Capitol against Early's raid on July 12, 1864.[9]

Ellsworth, Elmer E.
Elmer E. Ellsworth could be called the first Union hero of the war. As a young man from a poor family in New York, he lacked the necessary connections to gain an appointment to West Point, so he temporarily put aside his interest in the military and became a lawyer. While practicing in Chicago, he organized a volunteer company, clothed them in uniforms based on those of the Zouaves (members of a French military unit in Algeria, c. 1830), and toured widely giving marching and shooting demonstrations. In 1860, he entered Abraham Lincoln's law office and subsequently worked for his political campaigns.

When the Civil War started, Ellsworth returned to New York and recruited a volunteer regiment, again basing it on the Zouaves. On May 24, 1861, he and his men were part of the successful attack on Alexandria, Virginia. Upon entering town, Colonel Ellsworth noticed a Confederate flag on the roof of a hotel. He entered, climbed the stairs, and removed the flag. As he was coming down, however, the owner of the hotel shot him. The event was highly publicized and Ellsworth's body lay in state at the White House before being returned home.[9]

Franklin, William B.

William Franklin was a West Point engineering graduate from Pennsylvania. He accompanied Kearny's expedition to the Rocky Mountains, served in the Mexican War, taught at the Military Academy, and then supervised harbor improvements and other installations. In May, 1861, he was commissioned brigadier general of volunteers and commanded the First Brigade of the Third Division at Bull Run. By July, 1862, he was a major general and leader of the Left Grand Division at Fredericksburg. Burnside held Franklin partly responsible for that debacle and the charge shadowed his remaining military career. Later the Committee on the Conduct of the War seconded Burnside's opinion. When General Hooker replaced Burnside, Franklin departed, saying he would not serve under him. In August, 1863, he was sent to Louisiana and served there and in Texas as commander of the XIX Corps. While he was on sick leave recovering from a wound, the train on which he was a passenger was captured by Early's men. He escaped but saw no further service in the field. Leaving the army after the war, Franklin became vice president and general manager of Colt's Fire Arms Manufacturing Company.[10]

Gibbon, John

John Gibbon was a regular army man who is given credit for turning the volunteers of Henry Matrau's brigade into a distinctive fighting unit by means of strict discipline. He believed the keys to disciplining volunteers were "awards for achievement and penalties that hurt the pride," and it was he who provided the men with new uniforms that led to their first popular name, "Black Hat Brigade."[11]

Born in Pennsylvania but raised in North Carolina, Gibbon had graduated from West Point, where he then served as an artillery instructor and author of the army artillery manual. He was in Mexico with General Scott and also served in the Seminole Indian War. When the Civil War began, he and Battery B were at Camp Floyd in Utah. They were ordered east and were assigned to McDowell's division. Subsequently, Gibbon was promoted to division command and after being wounded twice achieved the rank of major general of volunteers and the command of XXIV Corps of the Army of the James. He was one of the officers assigned to arrange the details of surrender at Appomattox.

Returning to the regular army, he served in the West, where he led the expedition that rescued the survivors of the Little Big Horn and buried the dead. Gibbon later commanded the Department of the Columbia and retired in 1891 with the rank of brigadier general. He died in 1896 and is buried at Arlington National Cemetery under a monument paid for by donations from veterans of the Iron Brigade.[12]

Halleck, Henry W.
Henry W. Halleck was a New Yorker and a West Point graduate. He served as an engineering staff officer and authored books on military defense before leaving the service to start a successful business and law career. He also continued writing technical works, now on mining and business law. When the war started, Lincoln appointed him major general in the regular army and he was assigned to the Department of Missouri, where his excellent organizational skills were of great value. In 1862, he served briefly in the field and then transferred to Washington as military advisor to Lincoln and general in chief

of the army. Here his natural caution and attention to detail were handicaps in a position that called for bold planning and leadership. When Grant moved east in 1864, Halleck was demoted to chief of staff where he again served ably. He remained in the army commanding various military departments until his death in 1872.[13]

Hancock, Winfield S.
Winfield S. Hancock was a West Point graduate from Pennsylvania who started the Civil War as a brigadier general of volunteers in the Army of the Potomac. He advanced to division command and was promoted to major general of volunteers in November, 1862. At Gettysburg, he was in charge until Meade could reach the field and then led II Corps until severely wounded. Upon recovery, Hancock returned to service in battles from the Wilderness to Petersburg, where his wound disabled him again. Later, he saw active duty again at the Petersburg siege and then organized and commanded the First Corps of Veterans. In 1865, he led the Department of West Virginia and later the Middle Military Division and was promoted to brigadier general of the regular army.

Hancock continued in the service after Appomattox, advancing to the rank of major general. He was voted the Thanks of Congress, one of fifteen officers so honored. He was an unsuccessful Democratic candidate for the presidency, losing to Garfield in 1880, six years before Hancock's death.[14]

Hooker, Joseph
"Fighting Joe" Hooker was a West Point graduate who had seen active service in the Mexican and Seminole wars and then resigned from the army. Settling in California, he became a farmer and served in the militia.

As soon as the Civil War started, Hooker offered his services but was rejected several times before being commissioned brigadier general of volunteers and given command of a brigade guarding Washington. He advanced to division command and fought with distinction. In May, 1862, he was promoted to major general of volunteers; after Antietam, he was named brigadier general of the regular army and given the Center Grand Division at Fredericksburg. In January, 1863, Lincoln placed him in command of the Army of the Potomac, telling him that it was in spite of an earlier comment that "the army and the government needed a dictator."

Relieved in June, after the battle at Chancellorsville, Hooker was nevertheless voted the Thanks of Congress for his defense of Baltimore and Washington. He served in the West for the remainder of the war, leading the XX Corps from Lookout Mountain through the Siege of Atlanta. Later he served in the Northern Department and continued in the army as a major general until his retirement in 1868 following a stroke.[15]

Hoyt, Benjamin C.

Benjamin C. Hoyt came to Michigan from New Hampshire in 1829 and settled at St. Joseph, where he engaged in trade with the Indians and subsequently established a mercantile business. He was one of the first in the area to plant fruit trees and as his nursery thrived, his importance in the community grew. He held many public positions, including township clerk and treasurer, member of the school board, and member and eventually captain of the fire company. He served six terms as village president and was supervisor of the township in 1843–44. In 1856, Hoyt started a banking business, which was quite successful for several years and in which he was joined by E. C. Hoyt. He also served as postmaster at some unspecified date. In 1872, Hoyt moved to Mississippi but returned to St. Joseph, where he died in 1903 at the age of ninety-six.[16]

King, Rufus

Rufus King, the organizer and first commander of Henry's brigade, led it until his promotion to divisional command in 1862. From New York City, he was the grandson of a Massachusetts delegate to the Continental Congress. Upon graduation from West Point, King served in the Corps of Engineers until 1836, when he resigned to enter the newspaper business as an editor. From 1839 through 1843, he was attorney general of New York under William Seward. In 1845, he settled in Milwaukee, where he continued his newspaper career and served as superintendent of schools, taking an active part in local politics. In 1861, Lincoln appointed him minister to the Papal States. Just as King was preparing to sail on his assignment, Fort Sumter was fired upon, and he obtained a leave of absence and was commissioned a brigadier general. Having left the service, stigmatized for his decision to march away from Jackson's corps at Brauner Farm (see letter of September 13, 1862) and in poor health, he finally assumed the ministerial post in October, 1863.

King was serving in Rome when John H. Surratt, an alleged conspirator in the assassination of President Lincoln, was recognized and apprehended. Surratt had fled to Canada and then traveled to Europe where he joined the Papal Zouaves. He was returned to the United States for trial, which ended in a hung jury and his release. His mother was less fortunate. She had been arrested at the time of John's escape and was one of four people executed on July 7, 1865.[17]

In 1867, Congress voted to discontinue the papal mission and King returned to New York, where he served as deputy collector of customs. Suffering from continued poor health, including bouts of epilepsy, he retired in 1869 and died in 1876.[18]

Lammey, John R.

John R. Lammey, a twenty-one-year-old carpenter originally from Pennsylvania, enlisted as a private on April 26, 1861, at Milwaukee. He was assigned to Company D of the Sixth Wisconsin Infantry and rose to the rank of captain in October, 1864. He was wounded twice but returned to action after brief convalescent periods. He was wounded again at Hatcher's Run and died at City Point Hospital on February 15, 1865.[19]

Matrau, Benjamin Franklin

Frank Matrau was born on February 12, 1849. He enlisted and was mustered into Company E of the Twenty-eighth Michigan Infantry on September 30, 1864, at Kalamazoo, Michigan. On July 17 the following year, he was admitted to Harper Hospital and was subsequently discharged.[20] Frank returned home, and in 1871 married Mary E. Lamberson and moved to California, where he engaged in a mercantile business. In 1876, having disposed of his business interests, Frank entered the Theological Seminary at Faribault, Minnesota, and was ordained a deacon two years later. The following year he advanced to the priesthood and served as rector of various Episcopal parishes in the Midwest until 1890, when ill health forced him to Colorado for a rest cure. He then accepted a call to a parish in Englewood, Colorado, but later suffered the first of a series of strokes that left him progressively weaker. In 1901, Albion College, Albion, Michigan, honored him with a degree of Doctor of Divinity. Frank Matrau died in Chicago on December 11, 1903, survived by his widow and one adopted son.[21]

Matrau, Edward Newton

Edward Matrau, the baby mentioned in Henry's letters, was born November 30, 1860. He farmed with his father until his brother-in-law, Will Cook, joined the family and then enrolled in business college in Valparaiso, Indiana. Upon graduation, Edward returned to Bainbridge and taught for some time before accepting employment with a fire insurance company and later a bank. He was one of the organizers of the Watervliet Milling Company and helped reorganize the Watervliet Creamery, serving as manager and director of both for many years.

In addition to his business activities, Edward was active in township politics, serving ten terms as clerk and at least six as supervisor. While at the bank in Watervliet, he helped start the local chamber of commerce and served as its president.

In 1891, he married Alvina Endrick and they had one daughter. A year after Alvina's death in 1900, he married Lissa Van Vranken, with whom he had been associated at the Bainbridge Grange. Edward Matrau died March 29, 1934, survived by his widow and daughter.[22]

Matrau, Levi W.

Henry's brother Levi was born November 24, 1855, and died on May 30, 1886. He is buried at Byers Cemetery near the family home in Berrien County, Michigan.[23]

Matrau, Lucy L.

Lucy Matrau was born November 30, 1857, and spent most of her life in Berrien County. She became a teacher and worked in several schools, including those at Bainbridge Center and Bravo, Michigan. In 1884, she married Will Cook, who rented farm land from her father for several years. His main interest was in dairy farming and he was one of the organizers of the Watervliet Creamery. The couple had three children. Lucy Matrau died December 30, 1928, six years after her husband.[24]

Matrau, Morgan W.
Henry's brother Morgan was born on April 29, 1847. On December 29, 1863, he enlisted in Company B of the Twelfth Michigan Infantry at Kalamazoo, Michigan. Most of his service was in the western theater of operation under General Steele of Arkansas. After being mustered out of the army, he followed his father into farming, becoming one of the first Michigan farmers to breed Shropshire sheep.[25] At one time he owned about three hundred acres, which he later divided among his children.

Morgan was a staunch member of the Republican party and active in the Masonic Lodge and Grand Army of the Republic. He was a devoted Christian, and a church he built on the corner of his property remained in place until the 1940s. In 1870, he married Amelia Byers and they had seven children. Some of their descendants still live in the Watervliet area. Morgan died July 30, 1907.[26]

McClellan, George B.
George McClellan was a West Point graduate and had served with distinction in the Mexican War and then resigned to work as a civilian engineer. When the Civil War began, Governor Dennison appointed him commander of Ohio's troops. After the First Battle of Bull Run, McClellan replaced McDowell and had early success in organizing the army in Washington. His popularity led to his appointment as general-in-chief as well as field commander, but his methodical preparations for battle and his cautious nature caused repeated clashes with the government.

He was relieved of overall command but left in charge of the Army of the Potomac's Peninsular campaign. Its failure led General Halleck to give Pope command of the next major operation but Pope's defeat at the Second Battle of Bull Run brought McClellan back to his former position. McClellan was very popular with the men of the Army of the Potomac but his disagreements with Washington continued. When he delayed in pursuit of the Confederate troops after Antietam, Lincoln lost patience and replaced him with General Burnside. McClellan retired to his home in Trenton, New Jersey. In 1864, he ran against Lincoln for the presidency but was defeated. He did, however, serve as governor of New Jersey from 1878 through 1881 and was chief engineer of the New York City Department of Docks. His autobiography was published in 1887, two years after his death.[27]

McDowell, Irvin

Irvin McDowell was a West Point graduate from Ohio. He had served in various staff positions and was a major stationed in Washington when the war began. In 1861 he was promoted to brigadier general and placed in command of the Army of the Potomac. As such he was held responsible for the embarrassing loss at the First Battle of Bull Run and replaced by McClellan. McDowell continued to serve as a division commander.

In March, 1862, he was promoted to major general of volunteers and following a corps command led the Army of the Rappahannock for a brief time. At the Second Bull Run, General McDowell, now commander of III Corps, was censured for his part, having had the misfortune of becoming lost while riding to a meeting with Pope and was thus out of touch for an entire day.[28] He demanded an inquiry and was completely exonerated but never again served as a field officer. McDowell continued in the regular army as the head of various departments and retired in 1882 as a major general.[29]

Meade, George G.

George Meade was a West Point graduate; he fought with distinction as brigadier general of volunteers and was promoted to major general after Antietam. Just before Gettysburg, he replaced General Hooker as commander of the Army of the Potomac.

This change was not well received by the troops, because Hooker was still very popular and Meade hardly known outside of V Corps.[30] His failure to pursue the Confederates after Gettysburg was criticized, and although he continued as commander of the Army of the Potomac, Grant, the new general-in-chief, took direct control of field operations. Following the war, Meade commanded the Division of the Atlantic and then the Reconstruction district that included Alabama, Georgia, and Florida. He returned to the Atlantic Division in 1869 and died three years later at the age of fifty-seven.[31]

Meredith, Solomon

Solomon Meredith was the third commander of the Iron Brigade. He had led the Nineteenth Indiana Regiment until becoming brigadier general upon John Gibbon's promotion. Meredith had arrived in Indiana from North Carolina in 1840 and became active in politics, serving as county sheriff, state legislator, and U.S. marshal. He was clerk of Wayne County when the war began and a friend of the governor. His appointment to regimental command and his later promotions were based on politics, as were those of many others. His military competence was called into question at Fredericksburg, where he was re-lieved of command but reinstated immediately after the battle. Following his injury at Gettysburg, Meredith was unable to resume field command and finished the war as a garrison commander.[32]

He mustered out of the service in May, 1865, but was breveted major general three months later. Returning to his Indiana farm, Meredith later served as surveyor general of Montana Territory. He died in 1875. It is sad to note that of his three sons in the Union Army, two were killed in action.[33]

Plummer, Philip W.

Captain Philip W. Plummer from Prairie du Chien, Wisconsin, advanced to the rank of major in 1864 and was killed in action one month later in the Wilderness.[34]

Purfield, Henry L.

Henry Purfield enrolled in the army on June 15, 1861, at Beloit, Wisconsin, at the age of twenty-eight. He mustered into the service as a private on July 16 at Camp Randall. February 17, 1863, he was detached from the Sixth Wisconsin and assigned to gunboat duty on the western front. His death from disease at Cairo, Illinois, was reported in the muster roll for March and April, 1863.[35]

Reynolds, John F.

John Reynolds, West Point graduate and veteran of the Mexican and Indian wars, was commandant of cadets at the Military Academy when the war began. Named brigadier general of volunteers, he served in the defense force around Washington and then was appointed military governor of Fredericksburg in the spring of 1862. Later, while leading a brigade at Gaines Mills, he was captured but escaped to return to duty. Reynolds commanded a division at Second Bull Run and was promoted to major general of volunteers in November, 1862. He then took over I Corps of the Army of the Potomac and led it at Fredericksburg, Chancellorsville, and Gettysburg, where he was killed by a sharpshooter. There is a statue on the battlefield where he fell.[36]

Scott, Winfield

Virginian Winfield Scott was the general-in-chief of the army, having attained that position in 1841. He had started his military career as a captain in 1808 and rose to the rank of major general during the War of 1812. After service against the Indians on the western border he was named commander of U.S. forces in the Mexican War. During peacetime he compiled the first manual of arms for the U.S. Army. In 1852, Scott ran for the presidency as the Whig candidate but was defeated by Franklin Pierce, a Democrat. By the time the Civil War broke out he had achieved the rank of brevet lieutenant general. Despite advanced age (seventy-five) and poor health, Scott supervised the build-up and training of the federal forces until McClellan replaced him in October, 1861. He was one of the few officials who foresaw the need to prepare for a major war effort. His strategic plan of occupying the Mississippi River and blockading Southern seaports to force the Confederate surrender was ridiculed and termed "Scott's Anaconda." As the war developed, however, features of this plan were implemented. Following his retirement, Scott wrote his memoirs and toured Europe before dying at West Point in 1866. He is buried there, the only Southern non–West Pointer to remain loyal to the Union.[37]

Sheridan, Philip H.
"Little Phil" Sheridan, a West Point graduate from New York, was appointed colonel of cavalry in May, 1862, and within a week was commander of the Second Cavalry Brigade. A month later he was a brigadier general. Distinguished service in Tennessee led to further promotion, and he was selected to head the Army of the Potomac's Cavalry Corps. He joined Grant's Wilderness campaign in May, 1864, and in August, Grant gave him the command of the Middle Military Division and ordered the destruction of the Shenandoah Valley. During this campaign, Sheridan's personal bravery and dashing leadership earned him a major generalship and the special commendation Thanks of Congress. He then joined Grant and Meade on the left of the Union line around Petersburg and was instrumental in the final battles and in blocking Lee's withdrawal beyond Appomattox.

Following the war, Sheridan continued in military service, becoming commander in chief of the army in 1884. Four years later he was named a full general. He died that same year at the age of fifty-seven as his memoirs were being published.[38]

Sherman, William T.
Ohioan William T. Sherman graduated from West Point and attained the rank of captain in the Mexican War before resigning. Tiring of civilian life, he appealed to friends in the War Department and through them received the position of superintendent of a new military school in Alexandria, Louisiana (now Louisiana State University). In 1861, Sherman reentered the Union Army as a brigadier general of volunteers. He was assigned to the command of the Department of the Cumberland, then transferred to another district and given field command. Distinguished service followed and at Vicksburg, Sherman suc-

ceeded Grant as commanding general of the Department of the Tennessee. After the Chattanooga campaign, he again replaced Grant, this time as commander of the Military District of the Mississippi. In 1864, he undertook the battle for Atlanta and the "March to the Sea," later swinging north through the Carolinas to join Grant's forces.

Sherman remained in the army after the war, advancing to full general in 1869. Four days later, he succeeded Grant as general in chief and served fourteen years in that position.[39]

Wadsworth, James S.

James S. Wadsworth was the owner of a large estate in New York and active in local Democratic party politics. He switched his allegiance to the Republicans over the issue of slavery and volunteered as an aide to General McDowell when the Civil War started. Although in his fifties and lacking military training, he proved his mettle at Bull Run and was appointed brigadier general of volunteers. From March to September, 1862, Wadsworth served as military governor of Washington and that fall he was an unsuccessful candidate for the office of governor of New York. After Fredericksburg, he was named commander of the First Division of I Corps, which fought with distinction at Chancellorsville and especially at Gettysburg.

In 1864, Grant reorganized the army, consolidating several badly depleted units. Wadsworth was given the Fourth Division of V Corps, which contained much of his old command, including the Sixth Wisconsin.[40] At the Battle of the Wilderness, he was killed while riding his third horse, the others having been shot from under him. Two days before his death, he was breveted major general for his service at Gettysburg and the Wilderness.[41]

Warren, Gouverneur K.

Gouverneur K. Warren, a West Point graduate from New York, served on the western frontier before becoming a mathematics instructor at the Military Academy. He was named lieutenant colonel of volunteers in May, 1861, and fought throughout the early years of the war, suffering a wound at Gaines' Mills. In September, 1862, he was promoted to brigadier general and became chief engineer for the Army of the Potomac in 1863. At Gettysburg, where he was on the commanding general's staff, Warren saved the day single-handedly at the Little Round Top by hurrying troops into position at the last possible minute. He was wounded again and a monument honoring his actions stands on the hill.

When Grant reorganized the army, Warren was given command of the V Corps, into which the old I Corps had been absorbed. Later, during the battle of Five Forks, he was summarily relieved of field command by Sheridan for failure to move troops rapidly enough. He resigned his volunteer commission shortly thereafter, having been breveted twice for his services, but protesting his innocence remained in the regular army. Fourteen years later, a court of inquiry exonerated Warren, too late to redeem his ruined career. He was a lieutenant colonel of engineers when he died in 1882.[42]

Young, Smith

Like the Woodruffs and Matraus, the Youngs were early settlers in Bainbridge township. When Levi Woodruff came from New York in 1837, he bought property next to that of Isaac Young. Henry's friend Smith enrolled in the Union Army on June 15, 1861, and was mustered into the service at Camp Randall on July 16 as a private. He was twenty-three years old. According to his military records, he was detached to Battery B of the Fourth U.S. Artillery on September 12, 1862, and reported "missing in action" after September 17, the date of the battle at Antietam. The final regimental muster-out roll of July 14, 1865, states that he was killed in action at Antietam.[43]

Notes

CHAPTER ONE

1. Agnes Lewis, letter to editor; March 28, 1970; Henry C. Matrau obituary, *The Norfolk Press*, January 11, 1917, 8; Bernice Rudell and Catheryn Bishop, "Genealogy of the Matrau (Metras) Family of France, Canada and America, with Allied Families," 5, Maud Preston Palenske Memorial Library, St. Joseph, Mich.

2. Franklin Ellis, *History of Berrien and Van Buren Counties, Michigan* (Philadelphia: D. W. Ensign, 1880), 214–15; Rudell and Bishop, 3–4, 15.

3. Ellis, 215; Rudell and Bishop, 69.

4. Ellis, 348.

5. Rudell and Bishop, 4, 5.

6. Ellis, 223–24; Robert C. Myers (curator of the 1839 Courthouse Museum, Berrien Springs, Mich.), letters to editor, August 28 and September 3, 1991.

7. Lance J. Herdegen and William J. K. Beaudot, *In the Bloody Railroad Cut at Gettysburg* (Dayton: Morningside House, 1990), 64–66; Pension and Military Records of Henry C. Matrau. General Reference Branch, National Archives and Record Service (NARS), Washington, D.C.; Alan T. Nolan, *The Iron Brigade*, 3d ed. (Berrien Springs, Mich.: Hardscrabble Books, 1983), 284; Jerome A. Watrous, "The Littlest Captain in the Iron Brigade," Watrous Papers, State Historical Society of Wisconsin, Madison.

8. Nolan, 4, 17, 284.

9. Watrous.

10. Watrous.

11. Samuel E. Morison, *The Oxford History of the American People* (New York: Oxford University Press, 1965), 628.

12. Bruce Catton, *Mr. Lincoln's Army*, vol. 1 of *The Army of the Po-*

tomac (Garden City: Doubleday, 1951), 170; Nolan, 17–18.

13. Mark M. Boatner III, *The Civil War Dictionary* (New York: David McKay, 1959), 861; Catton, *Mr. Lincoln's Army*, 186–87; Nolan, 35.

14. Boatner, 552; John Quick, *Dictionary of Weapons and Military Terms* (New York: McGraw Hill, 1973), 307.

15. Nolan, 7–9, 12, 18, 28.

16. Nolan, 32.

17. Bruce Catton, *American Heritage Picture History of the Civil War* (New York: American Heritage, 1960), 369.

18. Nolan, 31.

19. Nolan, 39–41.

CHAPTER TWO

1. Catton, *Mr. Lincoln's Army*, 106–7; Nolan, 43–44.

2. Nolan, 44–45.

3. Nolan, 46–48.

4. Catton, *Mr. Lincoln's Army*, 17; Nolan, 50–52, 53–54, 292.

5. Nolan, 59–60.

6. Nolan, 61–62; John Selby, *The Iron Brigade* (New York: Hippocrene Books, 1973), 6.

7. Nolan, 62–63.

8. Nolan, 63–72.

9. Nolan, 97, 96, 98.

10. Nolan, 96–97, 102.

11. Nolan, 106.

12. Catton, *Mr. Lincoln's Army*, 48–49.

13. Nolan, 114.

14. James M. McPherson, *The Battle Cry of Freedom* (New York: Oxford University Press, 1988), 528; Nolan, 119–30.

15. Thomas L. Livermore, *Numbers and Losses in the Civil War* (Bloomington: Indiana University Press, 1957), 92.

16. Nolan, 142.

17. Morison, 652.

18. Nolan, 159, 160.

CHAPTER THREE

1. Nolan, 164, 168, 170.

2. Nolan, 170, 171–72.

3. Nolan, 175, 176, 177–84.

4. Morison, 655–56.

5. Nolan, 189.

6. Catton, *Mr. Lincoln's Army*, 178–83.

7. Bruce Catton, *Glory Road*, vol. 2 of *The Army of the Potomac* (Garden City: Doubleday, 1952), 85–93; Nolan, 191–93.

8. Nolan, 194.

9. Nolan, 196, 197.

10. Nolan, 206–8.

CHAPTER FOUR

1. Nolan, 210–15; Selby, 21–22.

2. Nolan, 215–18.

3. Morison, 676–77.

4. Catton, *Glory Road*, 199; Selby, 24.

5. Selby, 25.

6. Morison, 681–85.

7. Nolan, 223–24.

8. Morison, 677; Nolan, 228–30.

9. Nolan, 227.

10. Morison, 678.

11. Nolan, 226.

12. Selby, 28.

13. Nolan, 233–57.

14. Morison, 678–80; Selby, 29.

15. Nolan, 257, 365.

16. Selby, 29.

17. Nolan, 265.

18. Nolan, 266–67.

CHAPTER FIVE

1. Nolan, 263.

2. Boatner, 87.

3. Boatner, 552.

4. Nolan, 271–73.

5. Boatner, 919–25; Nolan, 274, 275; Selby, 33–34.

6. Morison, 689; Catton, *A Stillness at Appomattox*, 91–92; Selby, 33–34.

7. Michael Kernan, "The Object at Hand," *Smithsonian* (May 1989): 24–28; Morison, 689.

8. Boatner, 783–89; Kernan, 24–28; Selby, 34.

9. Selby, 34.

10. Boatner, 597–98.

11. Boatner, 842–43; Rufus R. Dawes, *Service with the Sixth Wisconsin Volunteers* (Dayton: Morningside Bookshop, 1984), 279, 280, 294.

12. Boatner, 162–65; McPherson, 733–35; Ralph Newman and E. B. Long, *The Civil War: The Picture Chronicle of the Events, Leaders and Battlefields of the War* (New York: Grosset and Dunlap, 1956), 2:92; Nolan, 274.

13. Boatner, 646; Catton, *A Stillness at Appomattox*, 176–81, 184–99.

CHAPTER SIX

1. Nolan, 274–75.

2. Boatner, 33.

3. Catton, *A Stillness at Appomattox*, 292; Morison, 692–94; Richard Webster, et al., eds., *The Volume Library* (New York: Educators Association, 1948), 688.

4. Boatner, 345–46.

5. Nolan, 276–78.

6. John S. Bowman, ed., *The Civil War Almanac* (New York: Bison Books, 1982), 225–26; Catton, *A Stillness at Appomattox*, 320, 342.

7. Boatner, 384–85.

8. Boatner, 900.

9. Catton, *A Stillness at Appomattox*, 331–33.

CHAPTER SEVEN

1. Boatner, 217.

2. Nolan, 278–80.

3. Nolan, 264, 277, 278.

4. Morison, 699.

5. Boatner, 674–75.

6. Catton, *A Stillness at Appomattox*, 352.

7. Boatner, 282–84; Catton, *A Stillness at Appomattox*, 346–48, 351–57.

8. Morison, 699.

9. Catton, *A Stillness at Appomattox*, 365–80; Morison, 699–700.

EPILOGUE

1. "Declaration for Widow's Pension by Jerusha Owen Matrau," February 13, 1917, Pension and Military Records of Henry C. Matrau, NARS; Rudell and Bishop, 5.

2. Lewis; Mary McKim, Affidavit confirming her brother's birth date, September 24, 1940. Copy in editor's files.

3. "H. C. Matrau, Former Norfolk Mayor, Dead," *The Norfolk Daily News*, January 8, 1917, 7; *Norfolk Press* obituary, January 11, 1917; Pension and Military Records of Henry C. Matrau, NARS.

4. Depositions by O. C. Hickman, DDS, and L. E. Bartz, MD, attached to Declaration for Widow's Pension, February 13, 1917, Pension and Military Records of Henry C. Matrau, NARS.

5. *Norfolk Press* obituary, January 11, 1917.

6. Chamber of Commerce, Norfolk, Nebraska, telephone conversation, May 27, 1989.

7. Rudell and Bishop, 4, 9, 11, 12; Ellis, 224.

8. "Mrs. H. C. Matrau Summoned by Death," *Norfolk Daily News*, March 28, 1928, 2.

WHO'S WHO IN HENRY'S LETTERS

1. Boatner, 79; Nolan, 17, 146, 197, 267, 275, 279.

2. Morison, 655.

3. Boatner, 107–8; Catton, *Mr. Lincoln's Army*, 255–57; Allen Johnson and Dumas Malone, eds., 10 vols. *Dictionary of American Biography* (New York: Charles Scribner & Sons, 1927–36), 2:309–13.

4. Nolan, 112.

5. Boatner, 216–17; Nolan, 16, 34, 91, 101, 178, 184, 196, 273, 276.

6. Nolan, 275, 279, 280, 281, 288, 290.

7. William Beaudot, "Captain Henry Matrau," *The Black Hat*, Newsletter of Sixth Wisconsin Volunteers, North-South Skirmish Association, Milwaukee (1987): 4–5.

8. Boatner, 244; *Dictionary of American Biography*, 3:391–92.

9. Boatner, 263–64; *Dictionary of American Biography*, 3:109–10.

10. Boatner, 303–4.

11. Nolan, 52–54, 292–95.

12. Boatner, 340–41; Nolan, 39–40, 50–54, 164–67, 291–92.

13. Boatner, 367; *Dictionary of American Biography*, 4:150–2.

14. Boatner, 372; *Dictionary of American Biography*, 4:221–22.

15. Boatner, 409–10.

16. Orville W. Coolidge, *A 20th Century History of Berrien County* (Chicago and New York: Lewis Publishing Company, 1906), 174; Ellis, 313, 314.

17. Boatner, 821–22, under the heading "Surratt."

18. Boatner, 463; *Dictionary of American Biography*, 5:400.

19. Military Records of John R. Lammey, NARS.

20. Coolidge, 681–82; *Alphabetical General Index Public Library Sets of 85,271 Names of Michigan Soldiers and Sailors Individual Records* (Lansing, Mich.: Michigan State Printer, 1915), 28:43.

21. Rudell and Bishop, 5, 10–11.

22. Rudell and Bishop, 6, 12.

23. Rudell and Bishop, 5.

24. Rudell and Bishop, 11.

25. Coolidge, 681–82; *Alphabetical General Index*, 12:106.

26. Rudell and Bishop, 5, 9.

27. Boatner, 524; Catton, *Mr. Lincoln's Army*, 51–52.

28. Catton, *Mr. Lincoln's Army*, 24.

29. Boatner, 531.

30. Catton, *Glory Road*, 261.

31. Boatner, 539–40.

32. Nolan, 183–84, 257, 266.

33. Boatner, 543; Nolan, 20.

34. Nolan, 267, 274, 288.

35. Military Records of Henry L. Purfield, NARS.

36. Boatner, 694; Catton, *Mr. Lincoln's Army*, 29; Nolan, 162–63.

37. Boatner, 728–29; *Dictionary of American Biography*, 8:505–511.

38. Boatner, 747–48; *Dictionary of American Biography*, 9:79–81.

39. Boatner, 750–51; *Dictionary of American Biography*, 9:93–97.

40. Nolan, 272–73.

41. Boatner, 882–83; *Dictionary of American Biography*, 10:308–9.

42. Boatner, 891–92; Catton, *A Stillness at Appomattox*, 349–57; *Dictionary of American Biography*, 10:473–74.

43. Military Records of Smith Young, NARS.

Index